59 Checklists For Project And Programme Managers

59 Checklists For Project And Programme Managers

RUDY KOR and GERT WIJNEN

GOWER

Published by
Gower Publishing Limited
Gower House
Croft Road
Aldershot
Hampshire
GU11 3HR
England

Gower Publishing Company
Suite 420
101 Cherry Street
Burlington
VT 05401-4405
USA

British Library Cataloguing in Publication Data
Kor, Rudy
   59 checklists for project and programme managers
   1. project management
   I. Title II. Wijnen, Gert III. Fifty-nine checklists for
   project and programme managers
   658.4'04

   ISBN-13: 9780566087752

Library of Congress Cataloging-in-Publication Data
Kor, Rudy.
   59 checklists for project and programme managers / by Rudy Kor and Gert Wijnen.
        p. cm.
   Includes bibliographical references and index.
   ISBN-13: 978-0-566-08775-2 (pbk.)
   ISBN-10: 0-566-08775-8 (pbk.) 1. Project management. I. Wijnen, Gert.
   II. Title. III. Title: Fifty-nine checklists for project and programme managers.

   HD69.P75K662 2006
   658.4'04--dc22

                                                                    2006023910

Printed and bound in Great Britain by TJ International Ltd, Padstow, Cornwall

Contents

List of Figures

Acknowledgements

This book could not have been written without the assistance of our clients who have repeatedly challenged us to find new ways of approaching their problems and offered us the opportunity of testing our methods in real-life situations. Likewise, we would like to thank the thousands of participants who took part in our training and coaching sessions, courses, workshops, start-ups and work conferences. Their interest for, criticism of and wrestling with our methods forced us to repeatedly refine and improve our ideas.

Although it is our names that appear on the cover of this book, *59 Checklists* could not have been written without the considerable support given by our colleagues working at Twynstra Gudde Consultants and Managers. Ultimately, much of what is written here comes from their experiences. We would also like to thank our editor Jonathan Norman. His thorough and detailed feedback on our different versions of the book frustrated us on many occasions but also helped us to make it a much more readable and practical book.

In order that our improvised way of working (which was not exactly methodical) did not completely take over our private lives, Gert is indebted to Paula and Rudy is indebted to Evelyn and his two children, Ivo and Lea. Their tolerance allowed us to spend several weekends working on our unique assignment.

Rudy Kor and Gert Wijnen
Twynstra Management Consultants

Introduction

Several years ago we wrote the first edition of this book to relate what we knew about managing projects and programmes at that time. Over the years, our views have found their way to people who are involved in one way or another in projects and programmes. Our concepts or methods are not only used by managers in different countries in the UK and Continental Europe: recently one of our books was published in the Chinese language.

Following the publication of the first edition, new insights have emerged on several subjects dealt with in this book and a number of issues can be better explained. It is high time, therefore, to bring this book up-to-date. This edition contains the knowledge we have gained and developed through experience of the management of projects and programmes. Even more so than in the previous edition of the book, we would like to emphasise that it's not the methods, concepts or the checklists themselves that can be useful and advantageous in project and programme management: it is the individual manager, together with those charged with the activities and efforts, who determine success or failure.

What examples are there of typical projects and programmes?

- gaining an ISO certificate;
- developing and implementing a new automated system;
- introducing new legislation;
- developing and launching a new product or service;
- designing and implementing a new process;
- introducing a new house style;
- launching an energy and efficiency improvement initiative;
- revitalising a neighbourhood.

Over the past 30 years, we have devoted much of our working lives to collaborating with clients, project and programme managers, and their staff to improve our understanding of unique assignments. Our inspiration was the key mantra of every manager: to get things done *for* and *by* people.

Our methods are based on more then 30 years of hands-on experience.

This book is written by two management consultants and is characterised by our need to classify, order and pass on knowledge, a perspective that is not always shared by managers, where action and pragmatism are often more important; these are two aspects that are often at odds with reflection and conceptualisation. Experience has taught us that neither of us are born managers. Happily, not all managers are born consultants, although both skills are needed for projects and programmes.

Since the seventies, our bureau Twynstra Gudde Consultants and Managers, which employs some 500 people, has dedicated itself to the professionalisation of project management. Thanks to our close association with the building and construction industry; the computer and software industry, which at the time was in its infancy; but also the electronics industry; local, provincial and national government; various not-for-profit organisations and branches; and our constant involvement in organisation change processes, our approach soon became a benchmark.

Twynstra Project Management evolved to accommodate both capital-intensive and capital-deficient projects, from projects where only a few people are involved to projects with an army of full-time workers. It has been adapted for projects that have a tangible end result and also for projects that are more at home in the world of ideas. The disadvantage of this is that the method is not really tailored to any one specific type of project. The task of adapting the ideas is left up to the project manager.

Culture counts.

About 20 years ago, the complexity of certain assignments made us realise that no matter how good project management was, we needed an additional approach. We called this Twynstra Programme Management.

With more than 30 years of experience in project management and 20 years in programme management, we have seen evidence that these methods have helped in the management of projects and programmes throughout northern Europe. We should qualify this by mentioning that our methods contain, quite naturally, elements specific to this northern culture – the difference for example in the way people respond to and treat power. This difference between the project owner and the project or programme manager must not be too great. Otherwise you will lose the all-important consultation moments and the relationship will become hierarchical, within which any criticism from the project or programme manager will be regarded as a form of insubordination.

The 'mañana' attitude of some cultures does not exactly stimulate a more planned approach to working; nor does the absolute belief, held by a decreasing number of cultures, that planning is not the way forward.

Too much ego-tripping does a project or programme no good at all; it must be a team effort. But having a team where conflicts are not aired is not healthy either, because there will always be conflict situations in the course of such unique assignments. After all, there are no well-trodden paths to fall back on.

WHY SHOULD YOU NOT READ THIS BOOK?

Many projects and programmes can be carried out using the management method par excellence: intuition, with the motto, We Will Wait And See What Happens. If you are happy with this approach, it will not really be worth your while reading this book. You will probably gain more insight and inspiration from books such as De Bono on the subject of thinking, *Alice in Wonderland*, *Murphy's Law*, *Baron von Münchhausen* and *The Tao of Pooh*.

This book is also not the book of choice for people looking for a scientific foundation to project and programme management: it is too practically oriented for this purpose.

If you are looking for techniques to help you with financial calculations, time management, network planning, quality control, comparative studies of software packages or the latest information about coaching team members, you would be better advised to put this book to one side, since these subjects are not covered.

If you have absolutely nothing to do with a project or programme at this time, the book will certainly add to your general knowledge. But the book is designed as a handbook and not a work of academic interest, so your time might be better employed on something else.

WHY SHOULD YOU READ THIS BOOK?

This book is aimed at people who, in one way or another, are involved or are about to become involved in a project or programme.

If your organisation works professionally on projects and programmes, but you have the feeling that this could be improved, this book will offer you suggestions. If you have any doubts about the suitability of your own professional approach to managing projects and programmes or feel that it could be improved, this book can help you to address these issues.

It makes no difference if you work for a profit or non-profit organisation, in an organisation that makes products or one that provides services. It is also immaterial if you work in an organisation with a staff of 222 or one employing 22 222. It does not matter if the primary aim of your organisation is delivering projects (the projectised organisations, like IT systems integrators, aerospace, building and construction companies), or whether projects are an exception in your 'business-as–usual' organisation (like banks and insurance companies, governmental and railroad organisations). Professional management of projects and programmes can have its place in all types of organisations.

The book can be read from cover to cover, but you can also choose to read about a particular theme, such as leading your team. You could concentrate on the checklists and skip the introductory text on the approach, but you would miss the context in which they are placed. Or you can just read the introductory texts, but if you do so you will miss the practicality that typifies the checklists.

We realise that reality is too complex to ever be fully reproduced in models, approaches, methods, systems or concepts, but we can't do without them. For this reason the book contains a large number of concepts related to managing, phasing, decision making, handling conflicts, leadership, and so on. We believe that these models are especially valuable for people in work situations who are confronted with the question of how best to approach their work

We deal with doing things right and not with doing the right things.

Concepts can only prove their value if they are used in practical situations. You will find that the concepts discussed here are immediately applicable to your work. If you are a project or programme manager, we will help you gain a holistic view of managing these assignments in terms of leading and motivating the team, mastering complexity and uncertainty, as well as embedding it into its organisational and environmental context.

In this book we do *not* deal with the process that leads to the choices concerning a potential project or programme. This is a strategic issue. We recognise the following steps in this process: ideas are offered that are based on the general organisation strategy; these ideas cannot be immediately routinely implemented, they have to be carried out according to a plan; these ideals are tested for their workability, relevance and feasibility (see Figure I.1).

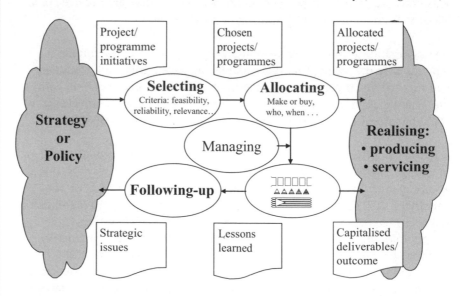

Figure I.1 Relationship between the formulation of strategy and projects and programmes

The next step is to determine whether to carry out the projects and programmes yourself or to contract them out, and to decide who does what and when. Only then does implementation take place. On the one hand this produces results and outcomes, while on the other hand it provides lessons about the way in which the project or programme was tackled and just how relevant the strategy was.

Strategic issues are then formulated based on what has been learned, which in turn are introduced into the next strategic meeting. But as already stated, these steps are not further detailed in this book.

In conclusion and in other words, this book is not so much about 'doing the right thing', it's more about 'doing things right'.

We concentrate on people and method.

Many general managers take the idea of 'doing things right' for granted, as something they do not need to spend their time and energy on. But they are wrong because strategy without implementation is irrelevant: 'Here is the fundamental problem: people think of execution as the tactical side of business, something leaders delegate while they focus on the perceived "bigger" issues. This idea is completely wrong. Execution has to be built into a company's strategy, its goals, and its culture. And the leader of the organization must be deeply engaged in it' (Bossidy and Charan 2002, p. 21). Our primary targets are, therefore, those who are interested in finding the appropriate approach for a specific task.

We would like to see project and programme management become more people-friendly, successful and meaningful and we hope that our book will contribute to this. In the book we describe what it means to manage a project or programme. We believe that we have created a readable and illustrative text, one that covers the subject comprehensively.

The structure is as follows (see Figure I.2).

In Chapter 1 'You have to choose the right approach', we discuss why organisations need project and programme management. We highlight alternative ways of tackling an assignment, such as routines, improvisations and processes, emphasising the result-orientation of projects and the goal-orientation of programmes. We define both approaches briefly.

In Chapter 2 'Organising for projects and programmes – the approach', the spotlight falls on the three people most directly involved in projects and programmes, namely, the project owner, the manager and the team member. We end this chapter by looking at the internal organisation, the key message here being that there is no single organisation structure that is better than any other for projects and programmes.

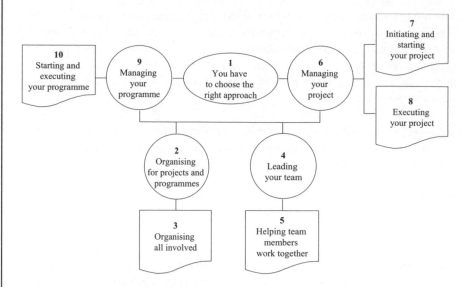

Figure I.2   The structure of this book

In Chapter 3 'Organising all involved – checklists', we discuss some checklists which can help you to fit your project or programme into its environment or context. The physical environment, the technology to be used, the financial means and the delivery and transport channels of a project deliverable or programme outcome, can be important environmental factors. Projects or programmes may involve many different players depending on their context.

In Chapter 4 'Leading your team – the approach', we deal with the interaction of people. We interact in a wide variety of ways, often through habit or because it's what others expect of us. Between the extremes of fighting and working together there are several other ways of behaving. Working together (and supervising this cooperation) demands an extra effort from both the project team and their manager. Those working on a project or programme often have no history of this type of cooperation: they have been brought together for this one assignment and will have to find a way of working together, including team building, leadership, conflict management and decision making.

In Chapter 5 'Helping team members work together – checklists', we present a number of checklists you can use when dealing with individuals who need to realise the successful completion of a project or programme cooperatively. This requires working as a team – something that some people would rather avoid. As a project or programme manager you can't provide *all* the energy and guidance for the managerial as well as for the non-managerial activities. But projects and programmes can only be successfully completed if managed in a cooperative way!

In Chapter 6 'Managing your project – the approach', we focus on the basics of the project management approach. We take as our premise *result-orientation* and the attendant need to define the (changing) project deliverable or result during the phases of the project. This process involves phasing, managing and decision making.

In Chapter 7 'Initiating/starting your project – checklists', we present a number of checklists to help you reach a complete and unambiguous project brief: the starting point of your project. Specifying this first baseline document is absorbing and difficult. In many cases a project involves a number of people and often includes team members from other departments or organisations. All these people have their own different language for (and experience of) projects. But at the end of the day, your project must mean the same thing to all those concerned.

In Chapter 8 'Executing your project – checklists', you will find several checklists you can use when the project owner has approved your brief; when the work that has been described in the brief has to be executed in accordance with the management plans and you are moving into the definition phase. You will have executed your project when the project deliverable has been accepted by the owner, made operational and all maintenance procedures and user instructions are provided for. Before this you need to complete the design, preparation and realisation phases.

It still remains a time-consuming business.

In Chapter 9 'Managing your programme – the approach', we discuss the basics of the programme management approach. Here, we take as our premise *goal-orientation* and the need to define the (changing) goals with increasing accuracy during the course of the programme. This involves programming, managing and decision making.

In Chapter 10 'Starting and executing your programme – checklists', you will find a set of checklists you can use to specify, to manage and to control the progress of your programme. You will have executed your programme successfully when the programme outcomes are accepted by the owner, made operational and all maintenance and user instructions are provided for. This involves the start-up, implementation and shutdown stages of your programme.

Finally there are a glossary, a bibliography, an index and a short note about the authors.

Project and programme management is designed to make things easier for all those involved. But this does not mean that there is nothing to it. Because a project or programme always involves the temporary combining of manpower, it is a time-consuming business. Time and time again, agreements need to be made with resource managers about the division of tasks, responsibilities and authority. You must be careful to avoid turning a structure that has been used successfully in one project or programme into the standard for all the subsequent ones.

People in organisations that want to manage projects and programmes in a professional way must be willing to reach new tailor-made agreements for each individual case.

Clear use of language helps to make communication easier.

It is also useful to have an idea of what has to be done at any given time, thus avoiding the necessity of starting from scratch.

Our intention is to help you on your way; what you actually say and do are up to you.

Rudy Kor and Gert Wijnen

You Have to Choose the Right Approach

There is something odd in our approach to project and programme management compared to a more natural way of working. People confronted with a unique assignment have a natural tendency to act first and think later – especially when it's an assignment that interests them. In addition, most people when they really want something tend to overlook all of the consequences, such as the real cost or exact specifications. In practice, this makes a professional approach to projects and programmes essential. Whether you are dealing with an extremely complicated technological assignment, such as building a tunnel, or a more cerebral one, such as a policy determination, the approach chosen must be carried forward in the proper way, not as an obligatory procedure or dogma, but as a means of helping people to work together.

At the start of an assignment, professional project and programme management is a lot less fun than jumping in feet first. Having to first think carefully exactly which problems have to be tackled, what your goals are, what the result must be and which paths to follow or, more importantly, *not to follow*, is an effective temper to your enthusiasm.

Project and programme management forces those involved to reach agreements on planning, tasks, authority and responsibilities before the assignment even gets off the ground – activities far more boring than simply launching yourself in at the deep end. But this initial investment always pays off in the end.

Within a short space of time it will become clear that when jumping in feet first, people's enthusiasm soon wanes. Feelings of frustration soon emerge: 'It's clear everyone wants something different', 'No one's exactly waiting for this' and 'No one knows what to do next'. The end result is usually a new set of frustrations: 'What did I tell you, we can never do anything right'. On the other hand assignments become progressively more fun when project or programme management is used skilfully, occasionally because a quick decision is taken not to go ahead, but more commonly because the results or the goals become clearer and appear to be within reach.

Regardless of whether an assignment is the result of a policy change, the introduction of a new product, launch into a new market or outsourcing services, in all cases it will involve drastic changes that require an appropriate management method. The choice of a method is often subconscious and may sometimes even be dictated by fashion. There is a great deal of confusion when it comes to talking about the management of projects, programmes and processes; one person's programme is another's process. This confusion can lead to an approach that's completely wrong for the assignment, with the result that goals and/or results fail to be reached, are reached too late or inefficiently; people continually pull out of the project or the costs become astronomical. To help avoid these unnecessary frustrations you need to decide consciously which of these methods to use.

Projects (result or deliverable oriented), programmes (goal or outcome oriented) and processes (action or interaction oriented) do not exist as such. You won't find projects, programmes or processes just lying around – they are not tangible. A collection of activities designed to create a unique product, strive for unique goals or initiate actions can be turned into projects, programmes and processes respectively. It is a conscious choice to call a volume of work a project, a programme or a process and to use the appropriate management method associated with each. This is the only way a manager in the role of owner or in the role of project, programme or process manager can do their job properly.

In this book we concentrate mainly on project and programme management. Process management is mentioned only occasionally and then in comparison to or complimentary to project and programme management.

MANAGEMENT IS A BALANCING ACT

People in organisations are increasingly expected to react quickly, flexibly, effectively, creatively and efficiently to issues and stimuli from their environment. For many years, the more traditional organisations of the major conglomerates such as the car industry, government, banking and the chemical industry, served as role models for all other organisations. But times have changed and they are no longer the only exemplars. Nowadays, organisational inspiration also comes from professional service organisations such as advertising bureaux, policy departments, think tanks, consultancy bureaux and the editorial teams of newspapers and television programmes.

Management and organisation is no longer a question of *this or that*, but sometimes *this AND something else*. A variety of developments are taking place within and between organisations: between an innovation centre AND a call centre, for example; at other times within a single organisation, the super-friendly front-office staff AND the excellent operational staff in the back-office. There's no universal right or wrong in this. The organisation and management method depends on the demands of the environment, management's vision on organisation, staff wishes and competencies, technological requirements and such like (see Figure 1.1).

We recognise several of these *and-and* considerations to be more specific to projects and programmes, namely:

- project or programme managers who can turn their hand to anything, *and* project or programme managers who have knowledge of the product, service, technology and/or market;
- projects based on energy, passion, learning moments and involvement, *and* projects based on rational planning and monitoring;
- programmes as a collection of activities managed by an improvising director, *and* programmes that are managed according to the relationship between goals and efforts.

This teaches us that there is no one ideal way to organise – not of the whole organisation, part of the organisation, or project or programme team. It all depends. But to be able to communicate with one another it is important to use clear, unambiguous terminology and methodology about how projects and programmes should be approached and managed. The *existence* of terminology and methodology alone is not enough: they must *mean* the same thing to everybody. Those involved must live the words and the spirit behind them instead of just slavishly following ubiquitous formats and handbooks.

Increasingly, we see assignments that by their very nature cannot be assigned to any one organisational unit (group, department, division) and cannot be executed in accordance with previously determined standard procedures. These assignments – vital to the organisation – contain so many new

	and	
• Management as a rank		• Management as a profession that brings fulfilment
• 'Upstairs' knows what is best for the shop-floor		• Management by the people closest to the process
• Bulk and long series, the 'pile 'em high–sell 'em cheap' mentality (at the expense of flexiblity and creativity)		• 'Lean everything' (at the expense of nothing)
• Structuring around tasks, division of work and departments		• Workflow around people and their interests and flattening the hierarchy by dividing processes as little as possible
• 25-year anniversaries		• Labour pools and temporary staff
• Norms and standards for the size of groups and staff/line ratio		• Situational handling in fuzzy structures
• Uniform organisational structures		• Hybrid structures
• Unanimity		• Acceptance of paradoxes, vagueness and search processes
		• Participative, inspiring leadership
• Hierarchical, planning and control management		

Figure 1.1   Organisational trends

elements that people in the organisation are unable to fall back on their previous experience. To be able to complete these assignments satisfactorily, you need to call on the knowledge of those who normally participate in other work processes. They are expected to leave their routines and participate in an assignment that is not part of their daily work.

UNIQUE ASSIGNMENTS CAN BE CLASSIFIED IN A VARIETY OF WAYS

People in organisations are regularly confronted with new situations to which they have no answer: a customer wants something new, the government introduces new legislation or the competition brings something new onto the market. Other causes lie within the organisation itself. Someone senses a new opportunity, a new product or service is developed or a new policy has to be implemented.

These new situations can be classified with the help of a number of dichotomies. A classification such as this can be useful when determining who is best qualified to lead those charged with carrying out this assignment. The classification of a unique assignment is also useful to staff them effectively, to determine the most appropriate method, to put in place the correct intervention method and to facilitate the carrying out of good risk analysis. Roughly 80 per cent of unique assignments can be classified using the four following dichotomies: stable or turbulent environment, concrete or vague assignment, adequate or inadequate ownership, and complete or incomplete operational organisation (see Figure 1.2).

Stable or turbulent environment

In a turbulent environment nobody really knows what will happen and what developments will take place. Parties often join a turbulent environment without warning while others pull out just as quickly. Coalitions between

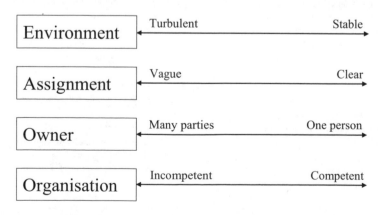

Figure 1.2   Several dichotomies to classify unique assignments

stakeholders come into being and disappear and financial sources are unknown. A turbulent environment is unknown and unpredictable, as is the amount of support for any assignment.

On the other hand in a stable environment relatively few changes occur at any given time, and any that do are easily predicted. The boundaries between the assignment and its environment can be described clearly and the assignment enjoys broad support.

Clear or vague assignment

The problems, goals or direction of a vague unique assignment are unknown. Many such assignments are often (politically) more sensitive because of the extra risks that the lack of direction attaches to them. These risks are the result of the techniques or the solution being unknown quantities or unknown technical feasibility. Finally, when the question of staffing and stakeholders arises, unique assignments are often vague because of their extremely complex character and long history.

In a clear environment the problems, goals and results are known quantities. This means that the outcome of a clear unique assignment is clearly specified, defined, feasible and achievable. The risks of a clear unique assignment are known and accepted and the assignment is feasible and easily managed.

Adequate or inadequate ownership

When an assignment is owned by a number of representatives from more or less autonomous parties, we can describe this as being inadequate. In situations such as these, each of the parties has part of the required authority, means and motivation – and it's usually the part that best serves their own interests. However, none of them is able to force the issue. This usually leads to protracted negotiations instead of adequate cooperation. In some unique assignments no one even seems to know who the owner is.

Assignment ownership is classed as adequate when the project is assigned to someone along with the correct tasks, responsibilities and authority. This one individual should have the authority, means and motivation required for the unique assignment. They are willing and able to force the issue. They also have the required competencies of knowledge, skill and behaviour at their disposal.

Competent or incompetent organisation

In organisations that are not competent for unique assignments there is a Babel-like confusion between the staff involved around the central goals, concepts and themes. The staff have little experience of cooperation but are experienced negotiators. They lack the knowledge and skills to tackle unique assignments successfully. There is little sense of urgency, only a tenuous bond with the assignment, fierce competition about areas of responsibility and little desire to think and work together.

A competent organisation for a unique assignment is one that is staffed by people who know how to tackle such assignments and have the knowledge and enthusiasm to do it. The staff have the skills and competence to complete it and are willing to work together. They also have a sense of urgency, understand the importance of the unique assignment and the desire to bring it to a successful conclusion.

Assignments that score more towards the left-hand side of the sliding scale for each of these dichotomies require greater improvisation. Process management may then be the more appropriate method. Programme management is used when the score is more towards the middle. Project management is used when all the scales are more or less aligned towards the right-hand side.

DIFFERENT WAYS OF WORKING AND MANAGING

Projects and programmes are characterised by their temporary nature, which makes it hard to fall back on existing tools. Unique assignments cannot be carried out using previously determined standard procedures. Unique assignments include: developing an information campaign, improving customer orientation, the development and introduction of new regulations, increasing market share, compiling a brochure for a foundation, introducing a new management system, reducing feelings of insecurity and introducing a patient follow-up system. They are also usually too important to tackle using an improvised approach. These assignments, regarded by those concerned in the organisation as important, contain many new elements making it impossible for them to fall back on previous experience and procedures.

Some organisations (such as architects, engineers, research and consulting bureaux) owe their existence to repeatedly carrying out other people's unique assignments. Other organisations are formed temporarily to carry out just one major assignment, only to be disbanded when that assignment is completed.

Yet other organisations exist only to produce exactly the same product or deliver exactly the same services year in, year out. This last type of organisation is characterised by routine processes, strictly defined tasks and that everyone knows exactly what their job is. This does not mean that this type of organisation cannot be confronted by new unique assignments. Imagine, if you will, the development of a new coffee machine, the introduction of a new information system or implementation of a major reorganisation. Project management, and in certain cases programme management, are useful tools for achieving these ends. But before looking at this in more detail, we will begin by looking at other recognised work forms.

There are various possible approaches to working of which improvisation and routine – seldom to be found in their pure form – can be considered the extremes on a sliding scale (see Figure 1.3).

Routine work is characterised by repetition

Both the result and the activities necessary to achieve it are predictable, because this is not the first time that 'something like this' has been carried out. A routine approach is most suitable if a certain result must be achieved repeatedly under identical circumstances and with identical resources. The most important advantage of the routine approach is that it enables efficiency.

Improvisation scores low on efficiency

Where flexibility is concerned, the methods are diametrically opposed: flexibility is the strength of improvisation. This approach typically goes with novel actions, with both unpredictable activities and/or results. Improvisation is often inevitable if you do not know the product/output of the work that has to be done. An improvisational approach to a problem is most logical if an entirely new activity is involved that has to be carried out under new circumstances.

Confusion: is it a project, a process or a programme?

Project and programme management are hybrid forms. Depending upon the nature of the problem, the situation and the preferences of the employees who will have to carry out the actual work, the characteristics of the various work forms can be positively or negatively valued. It is important that those involved recognise how the work is being approached because they will need to adjust their management of it accordingly.

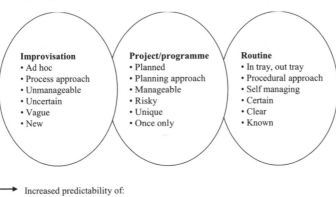

Figure 1.3   Three different approaches to working

To many, project, programme and process are synonymous; as are project management, programme management and process management. To clearly demonstrate the difference between process, programme and project, Figure 1.4 illustrates the characteristics of the three approaches.

BASIC PRINCIPLES IN THE MANAGEMENT OF PROJECTS AND PROGRAMMES

To be able to carry out projects and programmes, people will have to work together in ways they may never have done so before. You will need to make unique agreements about how you will work together. Someone who is just 'a member of staff' can suddenly find themselves in the role of project leader.

In organisations where many projects are being carried out simultaneously, the same person can be a member of the project team in one project, project leader in another and project administrator in yet another. This puts them in a variety of relationships with direct bosses and colleagues. Agreements are necessary to regulate these different relationships.

Project and programme management are useful tools for managers and staff, enabling them to direct each others efforts and energy towards achieving a project deliverable and to strive for the goals in a programme. Those working in projects or programmes are offered a new perspective, one which makes the why and the wherefore of the work clearer and more easily communicable for everyone.

Object / Aspect	Process	Programme	Project
Time line	Temporary, the end cannot be predicted	Temporary, stops as soon as possible and necessary	Finite, predetermined
Where aimed at	Possible/impossible next step	Predetermined goals	Predetermined deliverable
Decision making	Ad hoc, as soon as possible	At certain times, based on programme plans	Per phase, based on decision documents
Plan	Only present step is anticipated	Planned in coherent efforts	Phased in logical activities
Outcome	Depends, uncertain, possible	Unique, coherent, dynamic, desired	Unique, once-only, complex, desired
Players' attitude to cooperation	We do not know (yet) if we are going to cooperate	We are willing to cooperate	We have to cooperate
Management	By facilitating or stopping	By tempo, flexibility, efficiency, feasibility and goal-orientation	By time, money, quality, information and organisation

Figure 1.4   Project, programme and process: what are you talking about?

Only when a direction has been determined and a plan been drawn up can the activities be managed. The project and programme approach also provides the necessary language, rules of the game and tools to do this. Managing in the language of projects and programmes is always aimed towards the future. Plans are an essential means of communication in projects and programmes. Using a plan as a method of management implies: 'We agree to all stick to the plan, but the most important aspect is that if we think that we will need to deviate from it, we will only do so if the decision has been a joint one.' In this way, when necessary, the plan will be reliably revitalised and adjusted without ever losing sight of the deliverable, outcome and goals being pursued.

It is important to give explicit attention to the decision-making process of projects and programmes. When making decisions on routine matters the organisation can fall back on formal and informal procedures. But projects and programmes are unique. The people involved may have never before carried out these activities in this field with this combination of people. By definition, in each new project and each new programme the decision will have to be taken as to who decides what and what the consequences of this decision will be.

PROJECTS AND PROGRAMMES AS ARTIFICIAL CONSTRUCTS

Projects and programmes are collective activities, the former deliverable-oriented or result-oriented and the latter goal-oriented or outcome-oriented; they do not exist as such. Projects or programmes can be created from a collection of activities or efforts that are required to produce a unique result, or pursue a unique set of goals (respectively). Calling a number of activities a project or a programme is a conscious choice. There are some people who never get any further than this. They continue to work in the same old way and only call something a project or a programme to give it priority over other activities. Others realise and accept the consequences that choosing to work in this way really means.

Projects: the end product counts

This definition contains two key concepts, both of which must be wholly or partially new and unique: deliverable and activities. The most important of these is the deliverable (also known as the result, product or service) that must be achieved. The work necessary to do this is of secondary importance. This speaks for itself, because if the deliverable that is aimed for is not clear, it is already a waste of time and effort making an inventory of the activities, let alone starting them.

The project method is made up of three linked processes: phasing, managing and decision making. Each process is aimed at making the end result even

A project is a unique result or deliverable that has been collectively agreed in advance by the stakeholders and that must be realised with set means and through a unique combination of activities.

clearer (directing and bundling energy) and encouraging and making it easier for those involved to work together (univocality, clear roles, rules of the game and careful decision making). The project method starts by finding out exactly what result has to be achieved; the 'why' (the goals being pursued or the problems to be solved), the 'what' (the result that will be achieved, when the project is completed) and the 'what not' of the project (defining the relevant boundaries).

In the Body of Knowledge of the Association of Project Management (APM) in the UK, project management is defined as 'the discipline of managing projects successfully... It provides the single point of integrative responsibility, needed to ensure that everything on the project is managed effectively to ensure a successful project deliverable'.

Programmes: it's all about goals

Whereas the aim of a project is the realisation of a previously determined deliverable, result or product, a programme pursues multiple, sometimes even conflicting goals. This means that project management is fundamentally different from managing a programme.

A programme is a unique complex of goal-oriented efforts, including projects, which must be carried out with limited means.

The key concepts in this definition are efforts and goal-orientation. In this context, efforts and activities are both synonymous. Routines, improvisations and projects are all efforts that could be equally at home in a programme. The number of projects is usually very low during the start-up stage of a programme, increases during the implementation stage, only to decrease again in the shutdown stage. Improvisations are usually found in the start-up stage and routines become freely available in the implementation and shutdown stages.

The programme method is made up of three closely linked processes: programming, managing and decision making. Each of these elements is designed to achieve previously determined effects (intended goals) and promote cooperation between those involved.

There is clearly common ground: both projects and programmes concentrate on directing and bundling the energy of those involved and defining the various roles and rules of the game as clearly as possible. The theme of each part of this method is to define the end product/result/deliverable or end goal/outcome with increasing clarity (directing and bundling energy) and to promote and simplify cooperation between the parties involved. In addition, although not identical, both make use of planning and progress-control processes.

In project and programme management, attention has to be paid to both environmental factors and stakeholders, which have to be mapped out for each individual assignment. For every stakeholder involved, it is important to identify what their interest in the assignment is and how they view it.

The realisation of a project or programme stands (or falls) with the cooperation of the people involved in it; their ability and willingness to work together constructively and their willingness to recognise conflicts and to solve them harmoniously.

In the APM's Body of Knowledge in the UK, programme management is defined as 'a collection of projects related to some extent to a common objective… Programme management is the effective management of that programme'.

DIFFERENCES BETWEEN MANAGING A PROCESS AND PORTFOLIO

Process management is different to project or programme management. In many handbooks and in many organisations, programme and process are regarded as being the same; wrongly, in our opinion. Part of the confusion is due to the seemingly impossible task of finding a generally accepted definition of what exactly a process is. The term process has different meanings in different areas. In the field of technology, for example, process means a precisely defined work method, procedure or phased programme (process as in business-process redesign).

In psychological terms, process means human interaction: from cooperation up to and including conflict (when combined with decision making, negotiation, learning and improvement).

An important characteristic of process management is the distinction between the content and the process. Content describes everything to do with the object itself; and its elements and aspects. Process encompasses every aspect of the collaboration between the various parties and between the players who represent them; in other words – interaction.

Process management is supervising the orientation and design activities, open and secure, to ensure progress to the next common step.

Elements that are a generally accepted part of process management are openness, security, progress and content. In process management, openness or trust is the basis of getting people to work together. In the absence of this element people will resort to obstructive behaviour more quickly or will have nothing to do with one another. A feeling of security is essential to avoid parties holding back essential information out of fear that the other parties will use it for their own ends or leak it. If there is no progress in a process it will soon peter out. Tangible progress gives those involved the energy to continue. The content of the project, the object that makes collaboration necessary in the first place, must have something for everyone.

The core activities of process management are orientation, design and supervision. These core activities are repetitive and are carried out either as a divergent or convergent series.

Orientation focuses on finding an answer to the core question: What are the interests of the various parties or potential parties? It is necessary to check the impressions that individuals and groups have of themselves and each other. These activities provide vital information when taking a generally accepted, well-founded and well-documented decision as to whether or not to proceed to the next step.

Design is concerned with answering the core question: Which approach has the best chance of success? For example, should the approach concentrate more on cooperation than negotiation? If everything goes according to plan, this will result in an accepted, solidly-based, documented decision whether to start the next process step.

Supervision looks for an answer to the core question: How do the chosen parties and subsequent process step ensure success? Supervision also entails ensuring that agreements are honoured; that the process is carried out within the chosen environment. Last but not least, supervision is about ensuring a generally accepted, well-founded and documented decision.

Multi-project and portfolio management differ from programme management.

The only important element linking the projects of multi-project management is that their simultaneous realisation by the same resource (department, company, organisation, branch, unit, network) makes specific demands on the management of this resource. This makes multi-project management completely different to programme management. Multi-project management is also known as 'enterprise project management'.

Multi-project management (MPM) is managing a large number of unrelated projects simultaneously, all of which are carried out by the same resource.

In the APM's Body of Knowledge in the UK, portfolio management is defined as 'the management of a number of projects that do not share a common objective'. An example of this would be the operations manager of a company managing several different projects for different clients. Both Programme Managers and Portfolio Managers share similar problems of resource allocation and management'.

The central MPM processes are: project acquisition and acceptance, allocation and prioritisation, and realisation and resource management.

Project acquisition and acceptance involves taking on responsibilities. The organisation must have methods in place to be able to assess quickly and accurately if these responsibilities are acceptable and can be met.

Allocation and prioritisation entails knowing who, when, with whom, for whom, at what cost, with what overheads (on the basis of which specifications and which procedures to deal with changes) is going to carry out the project.

Realisation and resource management. The realisation of the contracted projects is the reason for starting all this. The way in which progress is relayed to the external client is often included in the contract. This is often preceded by an interim progress report.

YOU HAVE TO
CHOOSE THE
RIGHT APPROACH

CHAPTER 2

Organising for Projects and Programmes – The Approach

In most business-as-usual organisations, the question of 'who does what' hardly arises. Staff members feel free to use their own initiative to deal with things, or use procedures that were laid down, once, in the past. But in order for a project or programme to succeed, you need to determine the contribution of all those involved and the significance of the project for the organisation before you start.

The permanent organisation and the organisation required for the project or programme are interwoven but they both have their own specific characteristics with regard to structure, personnel, management style, systems, culture and strategy. Obviously there will be differences between the two organisation forms. This becomes manifest in the form of unavoidable and natural tensions between them (see Figure 2.1).

There are three key roles in every project and programme; namely the owner, the project or programme manager and the team member (see Figure 2.2). The team member is competent and enjoys their work and does what they have to do. You as the project or programme manager want the job to be done to obtain a project deliverable or programme outcome. The owner has the motivation, mentality and resources, and wants a result and/or outcome.

PROJECT OR PROGRAMME OWNER SETS THE AGENDA

In the normal chain of events, it is clear that general management is responsible for initiating and directing activities. General management has in the past drawn up procedures and guidelines that enable staff to carry out the activities with a certain degree of independence. The progress of this work is discussed in established groups, such as management teams, committees and departmental meetings. In the organisation structure, it is laid down who is responsible for what, who manages what and so on. All too often attempts

Permanent organisation	Variable	Project/programme organisation
Vertical Hierarchic Oscillating	Structure	Horizontal Coordinated Flowing
Activity-oriented Entrepreneurial	Personnel/management style	Result-oriented Concluding
Year planning Departmental budgets It could be better	Systems	Project planning Subproject budgets Good is good enough
Avoid precedents Routine Club spirit	Culture	Ad hoc reactions Situational Team spirit
Continuity	Strategy	Temporary

Tensions are natural and unavoidable

Figure 2.1 Some significant differences between permanent and project or programme organisations

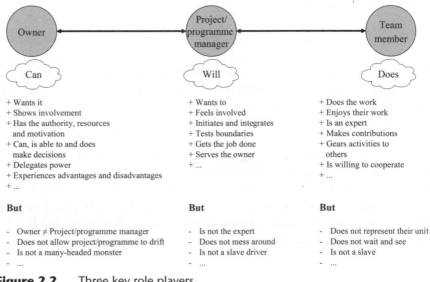

Figure 2.2 Three key role players

are made to fit a unique project or programme into these standard procedures and guidelines.

Projects and programmes are temporary affairs, which means that it is all but impossible to fall back on existing structures, procedures, guidelines and standard managing bodies. Amongst other things, this means that the owner's function and tasks must be interpreted separately for each assignment. There is often the tendency to give the responsibility for a unique assignment to one of the organisation's existing management bodies, such as a management team, the steering committee or the policy board. The motive for this sounds very plausible: 'We meet regularly anyway.' The advantages of using existing management and other systems as project owners must be carefully weighed against the disadvantages. The make-up of an existing group is unlikely to be designed for their participation in the specific assignment. Therefore, you need to consider carefully whether it makes sense to have the project or programme manager report to an existing body or whether it is more desirable, for the sake of clarity and engagement, to appoint a separate person for this specific assignment.

Projects and programmes demand extra effort from those who are charged with the function of owner. Yet many managers regard these assignments as being complicated planning issues that compete for time with their existing agendas. This results in them spending insufficient time and energy on fleshing out the role of owner.

Project owners are expected to remain involved in the assignment for as long as it lasts. At the start they must define the deliverable for a project or the goals for a programme, ensuring that the necessary resources (personnel, finances, tools and other means) are available. And the owner's role becomes even more important during the course of the assignment, when they need to manage the project or programme by taking decisions on time and making the choices that are necessary for its efficient progress.

The owner must make it possible for the project or programme manager to manage the work. Furthermore, at set times, the owner must see to it that the work is stopped and adjusted, or that it is continued. It will be obvious that the owner will and should remain involved for the entire course of the assignment and that their role extends well beyond simply the financial aspect.

If the decision is taken not to award the job of owner to an existing organisation, the question remains whether to award it to a group or an individual. Where possible, a single project owner is preferable because management unanimity is required. Frequent consultation is often necessary between the owner and the project or programme manager; consultation that in many cases cannot wait until the following steering-group, committee or management-team meeting.

The best person for the job of owner is someone who has a vested interest in seeing the problem solved or who wants to seize the chance offered. This does not necessarily have to be the person who initiated the project or programme, it is someone who will finally be on the receiving end of the outcome. Put another way, it is someone who can embrace the ups and downs of the project or programme, who can visualise the results of the choices made and who can put the deliverable or the outcomes to best use. A good owner is emotionally committed to the assignment and is willing to take actions and risks. They are people who do not leave a problem for someone else to handle, if the going gets tough. Committees and management teams will not remain so committed when their common assignment is in a precarious state. There is a good chance that everyone will expect one of their colleagues to bail them out.

To summarise: a project or programme owner is expected to:

- remain involved during the course of the project or programme;
- ensure that the project or programme manager is able to manage the work;
- make sure that the decision is taken at pre-arranged times to stop, adjust or continue the assignment;
- call the shots, have the last word;
- want the problem to be solved or grasp an opportunity;
- accept the profits and costs associated with the deliverable or outcome;
- be emotionally involved with the project or programme and willing to take action and risks.

PROJECT OR PROGRAMME MANAGER MAKES IT ALL HAPPEN

Each project and programme needs someone who is prepared to accept responsibility for realising the agreed deliverable or outcome. This project or programme manager, who may be a manager, team leader, project leader, chairman or programme coordinator, must be able to exercise the authority that has been delegated to them. This authority should enable them to plan all the non-managerial activities and have them carried out along the lines of the management plans that were drawn up. It is important that they enjoy supervising a team, coaching people and leading. In order to be able to lead people effectively, the project or programme manager must be capable of focusing their attention on the subject, the behaviour or the problem and not on the person. They also need to be able to stimulate self-confidence in team members and to anticipate when to take the initiative and when to give others free rein. Consistent behaviour, combined with a positive attitude towards others, goes a long way towards making up for a lack of communicative skills and gaps in professional knowledge.

The role of project or programme manager is not an easy one. It involves manoeuvring between professional expertise and people management, between ambiguity and perfection. And there are other behaviours and skills that need to be balanced (see Figure 2.3).

To a large extent your tasks, responsibilities and authority depend on the role you have been given by the organisation. It may be the necessary resources

The project or programme manager opts for:		
Personal power	← Versus →	Informal power
Belief that something can be made	← Versus →	Belief in natural development
Autocratic	← Versus →	Delegation
Independent ego	← Versus →	Serving ego
Patience	← Versus →	Impatience
Supportive	← Versus →	Steering
Rigid	← Versus →	Flexible
Manager	← Versus →	Leading
Facts-oriented	← Versus →	Feelings-oriented
Concrete	← Versus →	Abstract
Perfection	← Versus →	Ambiguity
Generalities	← Versus →	Details
Action-focused	← Versus →	Reflective
Complex	← Versus →	Simple
Today	← Versus →	Future
Verbal	← Versus →	Written
Good method	← Versus →	Good person

Figure 2.3   The project or programme manager balances behaviours and skills

are not made available to you and you have little or no authority over those who are working on the project. This is the role of a 'chairman'.

Only when you have authority over the staff that have been appointed to your project or programme, when you have your own budget and when you work to your own quality standards and information systems can you be called a 'manager'.

Whatever title you have, it is your task to initiate the activities. In order to avoid working at cross-purposes – especially with the project owner – you must also ensure coordination between the various parties involved. One of your main tasks is to make sure that there are management plans in place, with the necessary margins, to make planning and progress control of the project or programme possible. You may draw these plans up yourself; on other occasions this is done by the line manager. In the latter case, it should be made clear who is responsible for monitoring progress and how. If everything is clear one task remains: monitoring progress or seeing to it that someone else does this. In a small project, you will draw up your own time schedule and budgets and monitor progress yourself; in a larger programme, you may have assistants who do this.

You should be someone who likes and gets on with people. You must be willing and able to influence other people – team members, bosses, interested parties and others in your environment. That means exercising your authority and being able to communicate with people. It is essential that your attitude as a project manager is result-oriented, that is, delivering the service, product and so on. As a programme manager your attitude should be outcome-oriented, that is, changing the environment, behaviour and so on. In your business-as-usual job, activities are directed towards continuity; in a unique assignment everything is directed towards a previously determined deliverable

ORGANISING FOR
PROJECTS AND
PROGRAMMES
– THE APPROACH

or outcome. It is vital that you believe in the outcome, or it will be obvious to everyone else that you are merely going through the motions. You need to be emotionally involved with the work in which you are engaged, to feel that there is a point to it and that it can be realised.

As project or programme manager you should not only be a good judge of character, you must also be familiar with the organisation(s) in which the project or programme, for the most part, takes place. In other words, you need to have insight into the formal and informal division of tasks, responsibility and authority if you are to make the best use of them for your project or programme. Only then can you judge when something should go through the formal channels or when it can be dealt with informally.

You need to be capable of explaining, beforehand, to your staff and to the project or programme owner how you intend to tackle the assignment. If those involved understand this, they will know what must be done and how.

In small projects, you will probably do most of the non-managerial work yourself; technical or professional knowledge is at a premium. In large projects and programmes, it may be sufficient for you only to have a passing understanding of the terminology of the various disciplines, so that you can assess contributions at project as well as at programme level.

The tasks of the project or programme manager are often rather vague, as is the authority you are given. If you are to justify the responsibilities with which you have been entrusted, you need to be empowered to assign work to your team members within the framework of the agreed management plans. At the very least you need the authority to take corrective measures within the margins of your plans and agreements.

To summarise: as a project or programme manager you are expected to:

- describe the intended project deliverable or the goals of the programme;
- draw up the relevant decision documents;
- initiate activities or efforts at each phase or stage;
- act as coordinator for the various parties involved;
- draw up management plans for the programme or project;
- ensure that these plans contain adequate margins;
- make it clear who will monitor progress and how they will do so;
- ensure that plans are adjusted;
- be aware that part of your task is to keep an eye on the internal relationships within your project or programme;
- influence the environment and anticipate any changes in external factors.

TEAM MEMBERS DO THE WORK

A team is only a team when its members can and do feel responsible for realising the project deliverable, for pursuing the goals of the programme and for each other's contributions. (In Chapters 4 and 5, the characteristics and functioning of teams is dealt with at length.) In a team, the results of individual efforts add up to more than the sum of the parts. As project or programme manager you should play a guiding role only when it proves necessary. Team members need to be given sufficient latitude to confer with one another and take decisions according to the situation. Sometimes it may be the specialist who takes the decision, at other times there may be a majority vote and sometimes you should take the decision yourself.

No matter how the team is organised, team members are responsible for using their expertise to carry out the activities within the parameters of the management plans and to report (whether requested to or not) to the project or programme manager.

Besides their professional competence, the main thing that distinguishes effective and competent team members from ineffective ones is their enthusiasm, social intelligence and active involvement in realising the project or programme. The first rule of a team worker is: Latitude is down to self-management; take the initiative and know when to ask for assistance from colleagues or from the project or programme manager. Well-functioning team members will appreciate it if they are delegated tasks and responsibilities, and given the authority that corresponds to their level of competence. They will need to learn to live with the 'employee's paradox': on the one hand, they should feel as if they are a project or programme manager's equal, on the other they must recognise the difference in roles and responsibilities between themselves and their project or programme manager.

Another characteristic of team members is that they are involved with their own work goals and ambitions as well as with those of the project or programme. Irrespective of the nature of the project or programme, it is important that they fully commit themselves to the task that the team has to tackle. They must have good communication skills and be able to share responsibilities and authority with others. The readiness to accept help and to help others is also important. Bringing an assignment to a successful conclusion involves team members working within a relatively informal framework.

Few team members will relish this informality. But in order to be able to function well in a team, they must have a certain amount of skill in reading management plans and be prepared to work against a specific deadline with limited resources.

Team members may well find themselves reporting to several bosses apart from their project or programme manager. There are probably few team members who do not spend part of their time working in a permanent organisation – the organisation (the division, section, group, unit or department) that is their home base. In this context, their operational boss decides what they do while their functional boss decides how. In the permanent organisation the functional boss will also bear the responsibility for furthering their expertise and for monitoring the personal well-being of the team member, including holidays, rewards and the coordination of their performance appraisal.

It is essential that people who work on projects and on programmes are able to function when these three bosses are not one and the same person. Team members may be accountable to project leader A for the operational activities in one project, to programme manager B for the activities of another, while at the same time, the organisation structure requires them to report hierarchically to their own department chief on both assignments. To complicate matters further, they may receive functional support from an external consultant for project A, while being given this support by a colleague from another department for programme B.

To summarise: team members are expected to:

- contribute their expertise;
- carry out the activities according to the agreed plans and to report progress to the project or programme manager;
- to cope with the 'employee's paradox' – to consider themselves the manager's equal, while at the same time recognising the difference in their tasks, responsibilities and authority;
- communicate and share power and responsibility with others;
- be willing to both give and receive help from others;
- be able to work in conditions where the structure and balance of power is more relaxed;
- be able to work with more than one boss at any one time.

DIFFERENT APPROACHES TO ORGANISING FOR PROJECTS AND PROGRAMMES

The tasks, responsibilities and authority involved in project and programme management can be delegated to those involved in many different ways. Everything can be delegated to the management of the permanent organisation, creating a 'dependent project or programme organisation' (see bottom right of Figure 2.4). On the other hand, it is possible to delegate everything to a separate project manager, with an 'independent organisation' (see top left of Figure 2.4). The variations in between involve splitting power

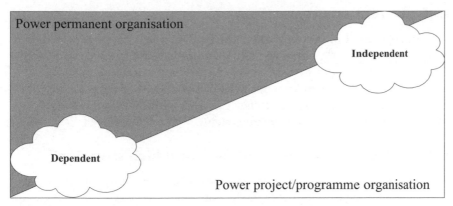

Figure 2.4 is depicted with labels: "Power permanent organisation", "Independent", "Dependent", "Power project/programme organisation"

Figure 2.4 Organisation forms for projects and programmes within a permanent organisation

(authority and responsibilities) between the management of the permanent organisation, and the project manager. Just as there is no general concept for structuring organisations, neither is there anything laid down for formalising the relationship between a permanent organisation and the one set up to realise the project or programme.

Coordination structure

Various structures can be distinguished in a project or programme organisation that is dependent on the main organisation. These include the coordination structure and the consultation structure. In the coordination structure, the project or programme manager is little more than a part-time manager and team members contribute towards the assignment from within their own organisation. You have little or no authority over the people who are involved in the execution of the assignment. This authority remains in the hands of the managers of the units of the permanent organisation or organisations. You merely follow the progress of those involved and keep them informed of the expected project or programme progress. Only the managers of the permanent organisation or the project owner are able to steer or adjust because the formal authority given to you is inadequate.

Matrix structure

A matrix-style of organisation has two alternative forms – one in which the managers carry out the consultations (they make no other contribution to the assignment other than to collect and delegate work for their employees) and one in which those involved consult with one another (the team leader calls those involved together for a meeting to discuss progress and to agree future activities). Whichever variant is chosen, the influence of the permanent organisation is not delegated to the project or programme organisation, often to the cost of the project or programme.

Independent structure

In an independent project or programme organisation, you are allocated your own resources. In some cases, you and the team have the necessary authority to bring the assignment to a successful conclusion. In others, employees are appointed to the team for a fixed number of days, they have access to their own financial resources and they can work with their own quality, information and other management systems.

Which structure is most suitable for which situation?

The *dependent* structure is the most suitable if what is most important is that the permanent organisation accepts the outcome of the project or programme and is not interested in managing it directly. Resources such as budgets are difficult to trace back to the assignment as they are shown as internal posts within the accounting systems of the individual departments. This means that the project or programme manager has no influence over the costs or budgets, as it is the department bosses who decide on expenditure. Even though you have little direct control, your informal influence can be considerable if you are well versed in the ways of the departments and are fully accepted by those involved. This means that an important task for you is to maintain relations with and between the departments of the organisations that are contributing to the assignment. Because a great deal is done informally, in order to cultivate goodwill you will need regularly to draw the attention of those involved to the fact that they are dealing with a team engaged on a specific assignment.

The *independent* structure is particularly suitable for important projects and programmes where the outcome is the prime consideration. The costs involved are apparent and those involved are accountable, since they control all the resources for achieving a successful project or programme.

PROJECT AND PROGRAMME ENVIRONMENT

Each project and each programme should be managed to fit the environment (or context) within which it will exist or in which its deliverable or outcome has to be integrated. Important factors include the physical environment of a project deliverable (that is, where it will be applied, how it interfaces with other processes and how it will be delivered). The associated technology and financial resources can also be important factors. However, most factors can be influenced by the players, which is why this chapter is primarily concerned with them. Many different stakeholders may be involved in projects or programmes (see Figure 2.5).

We discussed those most directly involved – the owners, managers and team members of projects and programmes – earlier in this chapter. Now we will deal with those who are less directly involved, which does not necessarily

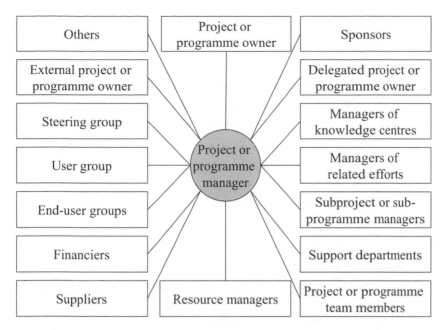

Others	Project or programme owner	Sponsors
External project or programme owner		Delegated project or programme owner
Steering group		Managers of knowledge centres
User group	Project or programme manager	Managers of related efforts
End-user groups		Subproject or sub-programme managers
Financiers		Support departments
Suppliers	Resource managers	Project or programme team members

Figure 2.5   Stakeholders involved in projects and programmes

make them any less important. People working in the environment affected by the project or programme often have a decisive role in the success or failure of a project or programme, if only because they are the ones who must apply or use the deliverables or outcomes, or because these assignments need external financing.

Their influence can be so far-reaching that it forms part of the constraints, legal or physical. Less far-reaching influence is possible from those who are involved in co-financing, supplying or those whose passive tolerance is required.

Everyone and everything that can or will influence the project or programme is part of its relevant environment. No matter how good the planning of an assignment, or how enthusiastic and professional the approach, it is someone or something from this environment that can frequently cause a deviation from the plan. People withdraw their support, they want more involvement, they suddenly want something different. The project and programme owner and the project and programme manager bear the primary responsibility for influencing these environmental factors and continually monitoring them.

Figure 2.6 illustrates internal and external players who can be involved in a project or programme. There are four categories. It may not always be clear beforehand whether a certain player will operate internally or externally.

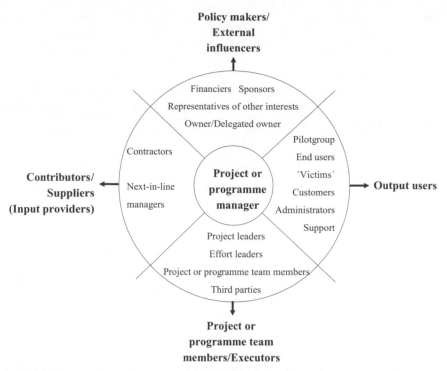

Policy makers/
External
influencers

Financiers   Sponsors

Representatives of other interests

Owner/Delegated owner

Contractors

Pilotgroup

End users

Project or
programme
manager

'Victims'

Contributors/
Suppliers
(Input providers)

Next-in-line
managers

Customers

Output users

Administrators

Support

Project leaders

Effort leaders

Project or programme team members

Third parties

Project or
programme team
members/Executors

Figure 2.6   Four categories of internal and external players

Policy makers and external influencers

Those influencing policy, ultimately in the person of the project or
programme owner, have a direct input on the rationale for the project or
programme. This means that they help to determine the desired outcome
– the 'what' of the assignment. Sometimes the function of project or
programme owner is delegated to someone. This person has the authority
to represent the real project or programme owner and is allowed to make all
necessary decisions within specified boundaries. There are three categories of
people who can influence policy: financiers, sponsors and those representing
other interests.

If access to financial resources is important (and when is this not the case in
projects and programmes?) financiers are vital. They provide the necessary
resources. Finance is a key resource, because money is used to obtain raw
materials, equipment and manpower.

External sponsors are especially important for projects and programmes. It
is they who can ensure that, where possible, the project or programme will
be championed. In all the networks where they are active, they can radiate
their support for these unique assignments. Whether requested to or not, they
defend the initiative whenever and wherever they think fit.

The third group of policy makers and external influencers are those representing various third-party interests in the assignment. Their attitude towards the project or programme cannot be described as being simply positive or negative. Some will exercise their influence to thwart the project or programme, whilst others will do their best to ensure that it succeeds. The representatives of interested parties and their intentions may not always be visible at the start of a project or programme. They can suddenly appear on the scene, perhaps in the form of an action group with a specific goal in mind.

Contributors and suppliers

Contributors and suppliers are also called input providers because they provide some of the means or resources to help the programme or project pursue its goals and realise its deliverable. Next-in-line managers are often asked to allow their people to do the required project activities or programme efforts. They do not fall under the hierarchy of the sponsoring organisation. Some of them may not, in an operational sense, fall under the control of the project and programme owner or manager and yet they also belong to this category; sister organisations and autonomous third parties can also be regarded as belonging to this group.

The involvement of suppliers can vary greatly for each project or programme. On the scale of involvement, suppliers or input providers can be put between the two extremes of 'anonymous' and 'partner'. On another scale, 'universal' is at one end and 'specific' at the other. If these two scales are combined, four categories of involved parties can be distinguished, as shown in Figure 2.7. In the course of the project or programme, a specific organisation that supplies input can belong to more than one of these categories.

In the *corner shop*, everyone can buy what is available. Nobody is interested in what the buyer plans to do with their purchase, and the buyer does not usually care who made the article. This is the easiest type of involvement for every programme or project and requires the least attention.

In the case of *contractors*, matters are less simple. Whether they are from the construction sector, the installation sector, computerisation, reorganisation or policy, contractors are known individually for each project or programme

Supply \ Involvement	Anonymous	Partner
Universal	Corner shop	Contractor
Specific	Research institute	Architect

Figure 2.7   Categorisation of input providers

and, if all goes well, they supply exactly what has been agreed. Because it is possible to choose universally applicable elements for a project or programme from a number of equally qualified contractors, great care must be taken to select the best.

The eminent and independent character of *research institutes* is often an argument for involving such an institute in a project or programme. It is frequently a question of getting the best possible contribution to the assignment where, beforehand, it was not possible to specify the output in detail. The reputation of the supplier must then act as a guarantee, especially in regard to independence. What must be achieved is then not what one of the parties involved considers to be the best course of action, but what is best in relation to the deliverable or the goals.

'Co-makership' is more complicated for the *architects* (designers, policy makers and engineers) than it is for the contractors. The architect is often the one who must specify the desired outcome in terms of goals, external interfaces, requirements or wishes, but even more often, they must devise the solutions that best meet the aims that have been set for the required outcome or deliverable specifications.

Project or programme team members

The project and programme team members include all those who, at least in an operational sense, are subordinate to the project and programme manager. This group also includes those who are also functional subordinates of the project or programme manager and those who have a hierarchical responsibility to report to them. In larger programmes project leaders and leaders of other programme efforts can often also be seen as executors.

Output users

In projects, and even more so in programmes, there are many stakeholders who use (parts of) the outcomes. There are subtle distinctions in their involvement, which can vary from, 'At last I am going to get what I have been waiting for', to, 'Everything that I have been working on for so long will be destroyed when I have to use this project result'. So these users include satisfied beneficiaries but also angry, frustrated 'victims'. These are often also intermediary groups who may act on behalf of the beneficiaries or the victims.

The pilot group is a body that is often used by the project and programme owner, on the user's behalf, to ensure the usability of the outcome. This group, delegated to guard users' interests, may represent them from the very beginning of a project or programme. In the case of large and, therefore, frequently anonymous user groups, the marketing department will act as their representative. In other cases a citizens' or users' panel may be consulted.

Those responsible for supporting or maintaining the outcomes of the project or programme are the final two categories of output users. Sometimes, they may be the owners. The administrators are those who must always know what the outcome is precisely, where it is and whose it is. Project supporters are people whose role is to take preventive or corrective measures to maintain the outcomes. There may be a special group formed to close down or dismantle the outcomes or deliverables as soon as they are no longer required.

Anyone involved in a particular project or programme can belong to more than one of these groups at the same time. For example, a supplier may supply goods without knowing much about what they are used for and, on the other hand, their contribution and how it is used may be critical for the success of the project or programme. Without the contribution of this 'partner', the programme cannot be successfully concluded.

All of the players can and will exert their influence on the course of the project or programme at different times. Some will direct their efforts to exercising a positive or negative influence on the course: smoothing, blocking, showing the ropes, interrupting, creating diversions, misguiding and so on. Others prefer to expend their energy on the deliverable or the outcomes: use, misuse, destruction, improvement and so on.

CHAPTER 3

Organising All Involved – Checklists

Your project or programme exists within an environment or context. It is within this environment that the deliverable or outcome needs to be integrated. The technology to be used and the financial resources are important environmental factors as are the delivery and transport channels of a project deliverable or programme outcome. Many different stakeholders may be involved in a project or programme.

In a permanent business-as-usual organisation, the question of 'who does what' hardly arises. Staff members use established procedures and defined processes. In order for you to succeed as a project or programme manager, the first thing you need to do is work out the contribution of all those involved. This means you have to get clear who is going to carry out which tasks, with which authority and responsibilities; it means you need to understand formal and informal power structures and communication. You also need to address risks or failure factors.

Checklist 3.1

Analyse the Environment (Factors and Players)

A variety of stakeholders and influences define the environment in which your project or programme will take place.

Most project and programme disasters, excluding natural disasters, are caused by stakeholders. Influencing factors can also influence stakeholders and both are significant.

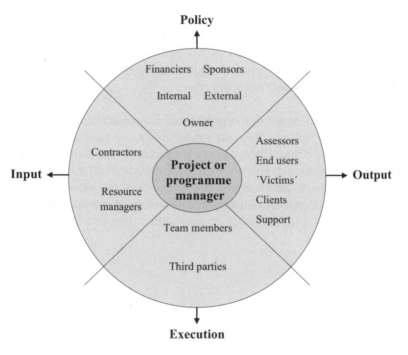

Figure 3.1   Ask yourself: who is or will be involved

- *How to analyse the environment of your project or programme:*

  - Identify all the relevant stakeholders.

  - Ask each of them how they see the project or programme, how much they know about it, how clear a picture of it they have; and identify the areas where they agree or disagree and the relative strength of their feelings.

  - Explain the goals of the project or programme along with any obstacles and ask for their opinions on it.

  - Discuss the extent to which and the way in which the interests of all those involved are addressed with your senior manager(s).

- Ensure that the stakeholders make it clear to you what the priorities are in (the parts of) the project or programme from their perspective or the perspective of their organisation.
- Determine each player's influence on a positive or negative power basis (legal/financial/charismatic).
- Look at existing and potential relationships between the players and explore how these may develop within the project or programme and the consequent effects.
- Compile an environmental analysis report and set out your conclusions in the management plan of the relevant decision document and/or programme plan.

Notes

- Compiling an environmental analysis at the start of a project or programme helps anticipate obstacles later.
- You may need to repeat the analysis if there is a subsequent significant and unexpected change of stakeholders.
- Every project or programme exists within this kind of environment.

Checklist 3.2

Organisational Differences

The permanent business-as-usual organisation and the organisation needed for the project or programme are interwoven but both have their own specific characteristics in terms of structure, personnel, management style, systems, culture and strategy.

Obviously there will be differences between the two organisation forms. And this will be the cause of unavoidable and natural tensions between them.

- *How to deal with tensions between the two types of organisations:*

  - Anticipate the differences and tensions between the organisations and their staff (for example different objectives, cultures, systems) before they happen.
  - Find out what the most significant differences are.
  - Deal with these differences by:
    - compensating for them;
    - ignoring them;
    - changing the organisation (structure, systems).
  - Gear the organisation of the project or programme to best exploit the structure of the permanent organisation(s) on the one hand, and the interests of the assignment on the other.
  - Record any findings – for a project in the organisation management plan of the relevant decision document, and for a programme in the programme plan.

Differences between business-as-usual organisations and project or programme organisations manifest themselves in tension.

Notes

- Look at existing tensions in the way people work.
- Avoid duplicating procedures in both the permanent and temporary organisations.
- Flexibility is a key competence for people working in projects and programmes as well as in permanent organisations.

Checklist 3.3

Most Appropriate Project or Programme Organisation

It is important to gear the organisation for a project or programme to best complement the permanent organisation(s).

This means paying particular attention to the division of power, authority or influence between the management of both types of organisations.

There are an endless number of organisation forms for projects and programmes, each with specific advantages and disadvantages.

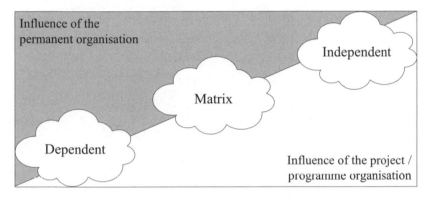

Influence of the permanent organisation

Independent

Matrix

Dependent

Influence of the project / programme organisation

Figure 3.2   An appropriate project or programme organisation has to be chosen

- *How to choose the right organisational form:*
  - Determine who has an interest in the project or programme and the nature (size, direction and scope) of their interest. Find out what the real differences in opinions are.
  - Acquaint the owner with his or her tasks, responsibilities and authority.
  - Appoint a project or programme manager and advise them of their tasks, responsibilities and authority.
  - Appoint the team members and advise them of their tasks, responsibilities and authority.
  - Set out clear agreements with all the interested parties.
  - Record information in the relevant decision document from the project's organisation management plan or in the programme's programme plan.

Notes

- Watch out for the 'not invented here' effect.

- A project or programme that is vitally important should be easily accepted and offer a great deal of scope.
- The organisation for a project or programme should be, by definition, changeable, but managed.

Checklist 3.4

Fill the Three Key Positions

There are three key roles in every project and programme, namely the owner, the project or programme manager and the team member.

Team members need to be competent, enjoy their work and need to do what needs to be done. The project or programme manager should be closely involved and needs to justify their role in the assignment. The owner has the motivation, authority and resources, and is looking for a specific result and/or outcome.

- ***How to fill the three key positions:***
  - Look for the right owner:
    - find out what they want;
    - judge the level of involvement they can offer;
    - check to what extent they can deliver what is necessary for the project or programme.
  - Select the right project or programme manager:
    - assess their competencies;
    - check that they are sufficiently independent;
    - ensure that they are up to the task.
  - Appoint the right team members:
    - assess their competencies;
    - assess their willingness and availability;
    - ensure there is a good climate of cooperation.

Notes

- Make sure the owner is not a many-headed monster or a committee of bureaucrats.
- The project or programme manager does not need to be any type of expert.
- The team members must not promote the interests of their 'department' ahead of the interests of the project or programme.

The three key positions of the project or programme must be correctly filled.

Checklist 3.5

Fill the Position of Owner

Before a project or programme can formally begin, it must be clear who is the owner. This is a crucial decision. More projects and programmes go wrong for the lack of or the wrong choice of owner than for any other reason.

The (delegated) owner is the person within the organisation who makes sure that the conditions are in place to enable the project or programme to succeed.

A good owner can and does ensure that the project or programme can be carried out.

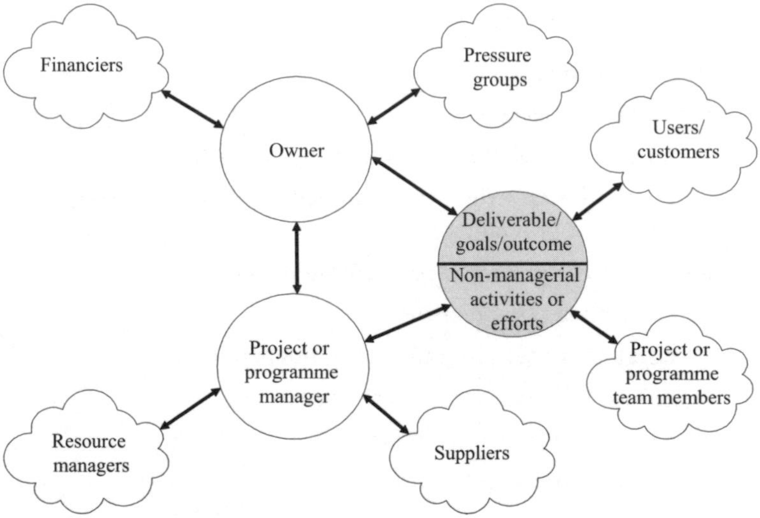

Figure 3.3   There are many parties trying to influence the owner

- *How to fill the position of owner:*

    - As a project or programme owner, your role is to make the significance and need for the project or programme absolutely clear to everyone, along with the benefit(s) that the outcome and/or deliverable will bring.

    - Ensure that you are in sole charge of the assignment, that you have the last word.

    - Stay involved and let everyone see that you are involved.

    - Ensure that the project or programme manager has the resources to carry out their work; do not get under their feet.

    - At the request of the project or programme manager or on your own initiative, decide whether to stop, adjust or continue the project or programme.

- Accept the profits and losses of the project or programme.
- Engage with the project or programme; be prepared to take risks.
- Let the project or programme keep you awake.

Notes

- If the owner does not ensure support the assignment will fail.
- If the owner cannot provide resources the assignment will fail.
- The owner's choice of project or programme manager will influence the outcome and the chances of success.

Checklist 3.6

Fill the Position of Project or Programme Manager

Project or programme managers invariably share responsibilities and authority with others outside the project or programme who are not necessarily more senior to them in the parent organisation. The leadership of an assignment is often shared by a number of people.

The people carrying out the work will often have far more professional or technical knowledge than the person leading it.

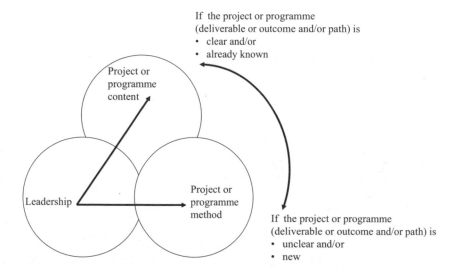

Figure 3.4   Each project or programme requires an appropriate manager

A project or programme manager is a person with knowledge in many disciplines but excelling in none.

* ***How to fill the position of project or programme manager:***

    * As a project or programme manager, you need to be goal-oriented (in a programme) and/or deliverable-oriented (in a project); this implies tenacity, ambition and independence.

    * Wherever possible, make sure there are not restrictive and obstructive procedures that could damage the assignment.

    * Keep yourself up to date:

        – leadership (managing and supporting);

        – the content (not too one-sided; be aware of general patterns);

        – the basics of project or programme management.

    * When appointing a project or programme manager, ensure that they have all the necessary competencies:

- knowledge (do they know enough; is their knowledge balanced in all areas?);
- experience and expertise (can they do what is being asked of them; do they have a proven track record?);
- attitude (do they want the assignment enough; are they sufficiently motivated?).

Notes

- You can't become a professional project or programme manager overnight.
- Never wrong-foot your owner.
- Always give your team sufficient scope.

Checklist 3.7

Fill the Position of Team Member

Only when those charged with providing the content of a project or programme feel a measure of joint responsibility can there be any talk of a project or programme team.

No project or programme can ever be completed successfully without motivated team members.

The results of all the team activities or efforts should be greater than the sum of the individual activities or efforts. The team members are the powerhouse of the project or programme; they are the ones who have to carry out the non-managerial activities.

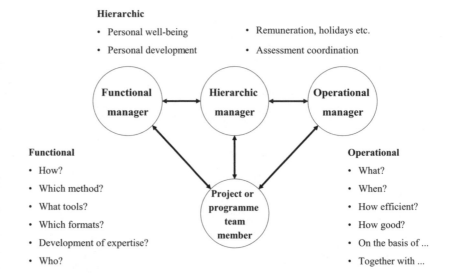

Figure 3.5   Team members have to work for many managers

* ***How to fill the position of team members:***

  * As a team member, your role is to bring the expertise the assignment requires.

  * You need to carry out the non-managerial activities or efforts, the boundaries being determined by the management plan.

  * Whether requested to or not, you should report progress to the project or programme manager on a regular basis.

  * Recognise the 'team member's paradox' – you are the project or programme manager's equal; at the same time you need to understand the differences between yourselves in such matters as operational tasks, responsibilities and authority.

  * Share responsibilities and authority by communicating with others.

  * Help others and let them help you.

- Avoid the need for rigid structures and power balances.
- Show willingness to work for more than one manager at any one time.

Notes

- If you don't do it, perhaps no one else will, but it has to be done.
- It's not about doing your best, but about doing what has been agreed.
- In a project or programme, the person who is the expert does not always have the last say.
- Waiting until something is noticed is an extremely serious transgression in any project or programme – you need to anticipate and tackle problems.

Checklist 3.8

Analyse the Failure Factors and Risks

Recognising and tracing failure factors and risks in a project or programme can be done in a number of ways. What is important is that it takes place. Before starting a project or programme, it is always worthwhile carrying out a failure-factor analysis, sometimes known as a risk analysis.

Risk analysis will help you recognise future and potential problems before they happen. The possible effects of disruptions can be quantified and estimated. You also need a contingency plan (a 'what if?' plan) for the main failure factors. Your margin for error or delay needs to be widest in the areas of greatest risk.

Best-case and worst-case scenarios are helpful for determining likely risks.

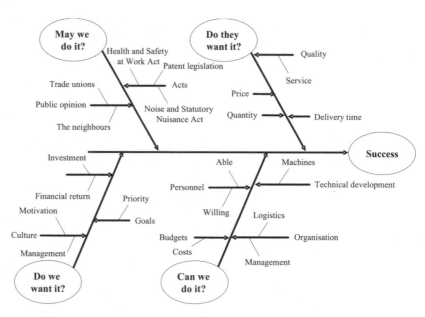

Figure 3.6   An example of possible risk areas

- *How to analyse and handle the risks:*

    - Set up a failure-factor analysis involving input from everyone concerned.

    - Find out if everyone has the same view of the project or programme.

    - Allow everyone to work out for themselves which failure factors could prevent the project or programme from achieving its planned outcome, prevent the carrying out of the non-managerial activities or efforts and hinder management or control.

    - Make a list of the jointly recognised failure factors and ask everyone to identify the factors that influence the likelihood of failure.

- Reach a joint estimate for each failure factor and then determine individually what would be the effects if each individual failure factor were to occur.
- Make a collective report of these findings and try (as a group) to find ways of solving, preventing or avoiding the most serious failure factors.
- Use these findings in determining the margins for each management perspective of the assignment.
- Record the final agreements in the project or programme plans and monitor the progress of these plans through the normal channels.

Notes

- Failure-factor analysis is aimed at ensuring the future of the project or programme.
- Following a failure-factor analysis, you should be able to answer the question, 'Are we ready?' with the response, 'Yes, on condition that...'.
- Do not rush this analysis; time spent now will save you time in the long run.

Checklist 3.9

Drum Up Support for Your Project or Programme

Do not take support for a project or programme for granted.

Support will certainly not be found among those who oppose the goals or the project deliverable. Make a careful inventory of the forces that affect the project or programme as the first step towards attempting to drum up support for it.

A project or programme is carried by the support that it receives.

Figure 3.7   Many positions between friend and foe

- *How to act with friends and foes:*

    - Make an inventory of all the stakeholders.

    - Assess each stakeholder's:

        - interests;

        - type of influence (positive/negative);

        - degree of strength (strong/weak);

        - openness to development.

    - Draw up a plan for developing support:

        - who will influence which stakeholder when?

        - how?

        - who can bring which stakeholders together, for what reason and in what way?

    - Carry out your plan, control progress regularly and review the plan if circumstances so dictate.

Notes

- The actual outcome of a project or programme is a function of the factual deliverable or outcome and of how different stakeholders perceive this outcome.
- Remember to help get your supporters onside.
- The project or programme owner will play a crucial role in winning and sustaining support.

ORGANISING
ALL INVOLVED
– CHECKLISTS

Checklist 3.10

Communicate With Your Stakeholders

Communication is one of the most important success factors for any project or programme. In practice, the means of communication are often under- or overestimated and projects or programmes are rarely free from tension. The complex environment within which the assignment is completed contributes to this tension.

The assignment is surrounded by people who all have vested interests in the outcome. Communication can help relieve this tension between the various expectations. Effective communication can help create the right sort of vision for the project or programme and offer a basis for understanding, trust and participation.

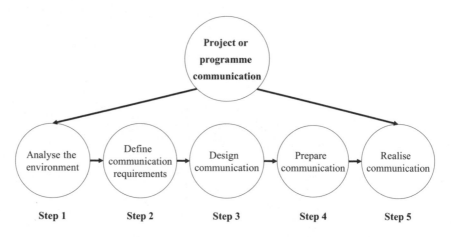

Figure 3.8   Communication can itself be handled as a 'project'

- ***How to communicate effectively:***

  - Analyse the project or programme environment.
  - Develop a vision of the basic principles and conditions needed for successful communication.
  - Determine the communication target groups, their goals and strategy.
  - Define the requirements for your communication.
  - Design means, messages and channels for communication.
  - Prepare your communication:
    - divide the tasks, responsibilities and authority;
    - ensure you have enough and the right people to do the job;

Even the best project or programme can be damaged by poor communication.

- determine the communication style, culture, means, channels, systems and procedures, and record this in your management plan.
- Realise the various communication activities.
- Control progress, adjust ... and/or replan.

Notes

- A flawed project or programme cannot be saved by good communication.
- Give adequate priority to communication and recognise its importance in managing the project or programme.
- Be on your guard against the whole exercise turning into a communication circus; word of mouth is also often a powerful communication tool.

CHAPTER 4

Leading Your Team – The Approach

The success of a project or programme depends to a large extent on you (as a project or programme manager) and your team. Those involved must have more than just knowledge of the subject matter; the chemistry between them is equally important.

The ability and, more especially, the willingness of those involved in projects and programmes are of fundamental importance. They have to cooperate; cooperation is necessary to bring a project or programme to a satisfactory conclusion. We will highlight the process, the human side of projects and programmes, based on the premise that it is impossible to complete such an assignment if little or no attention is paid to the process of teamworking. And the more unique the assignment, the more difficult this will be. Those working on a project or programme often have no history of this type of cooperation. They have now been brought together for this one assignment and need to find a way of working together. In this type of situation new skills and abilities come to the fore, such as team building, leadership, conflict management and decision making.

TEAMWORK IS MORE THAN JUST CONTENT AND PROCEDURES

The confusion about working as a team often starts at the outset when it is not clear to everyone what the team should be or do. When colleagues work together they may be expected to behave differently from situations where they form part of a group around a leader, in which instance the only thing they have in common is the person supervising the group. The group's leader is expected to provide all the energy and guidance. Just to be clear: projects and programmes cannot be successfully completed if managed in this way!

The term 'team' (see Figure 4.1) can be defined as: 'a group of people with complementary skills, dedicated to the pursuit of mutual goals and who use an agreed working method for which they take joint responsibility'.

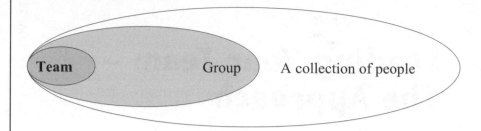

Figure 4.1   Not every group is a team

For years now, people have been searching for a scientifically based argument that can tell us what is the maximum number of team members who can still work productively. As yet science has failed to come up with the answer, but in practice, experience suggests the maximum number is about ten or twelve. The more team members there are, the harder it is to arrange meetings. And, even more importantly, the more team members there are, the more complex the interaction. A free exchange of ideas is usually only possible with a limited number of people. If the group is too large, it is difficult to be aware of each other (in a psychological sense) and the team members have less 'broadcasting time' available to actively contribute to the group.

Strange as it may seem, there has been very little research done into the minimum size of an effective team. Because team members must be able to take over each other's tasks – teams must not be left vulnerable if a team member becomes ill or leaves – teams should probably consist of at least four people. There are three processes at the core of teamworking: content, procedure and interaction (see Figure 4.2).

Content

What must be achieved? How and for what purpose has the group been formed. For example: how should you determine the goal or problem, deliverable specification? How should you clarify the method? How will you exchange information, or ideas?

Procedure

How will the team work together and how will meetings be organised? For example: what are your decision-making procedures? How will you draw up an agenda and take minutes?

Interaction

How will you cooperate? For example: what is your ratio of listening to speaking? What is the combination of verbal and non-verbal behaviour and how do you react to each other?

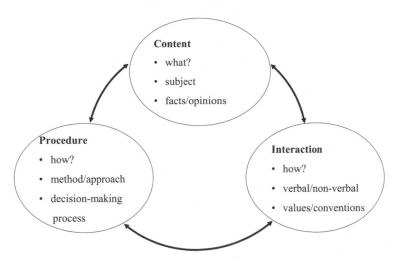

Figure 4.2   Working together as a team requires attention to three specific aspects

In most cases, the contribution of a number of individuals is needed to bring about the successful completion of a unique and complex assignment. In some cases, cooperation simply consists of keeping each other up to date by telephone, fax or e-mail. In other cases, team members tackle the assignment together. Despite the fact that working in teams is a regular topic of discussion, working with, in or for a team is something that a number of people would rather avoid. In practice, we hear comments such as: 'We are not a team, because everyone works for themselves', 'Working together in a team only slows things down', 'Just tell me what to do and I'll do it', 'When it comes to the crunch, the team manager makes all the decisions anyway', 'I am only a researcher, I can't work with anyone' and so on.

PEOPLE INTERACT IN A WIDE VARIETY OF WAYS

People behave in their own peculiar way often through habit or because it's what others expect of them; and also because they deem it necessary. The ways in which people interact are shown in Figure 4.3. One axis shows the extremes of 'people who know how to feel involved' (Involved) and 'people who find it impossible to do this' (Not involved), while a second axis shows the extremes of 'wanting to do something together'(Together) and 'being against each other' (Opposed). Involvement usually entails seeking contact and recognition from various interest groups and parties. At the opposite end of the spectrum are those who do not seek contact and who do not recognise or are unaware of the existence of these same groups or parties. Together implies parallel goals and mutual trust, as opposed to people who do not trust each other and who are pursuing conflicting goals.

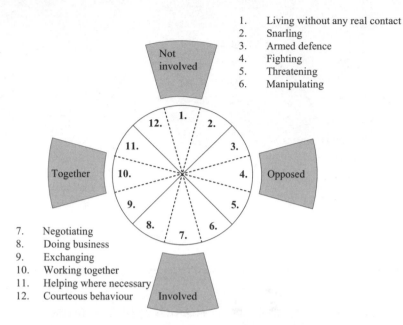

1. Living without any real contact
2. Snarling
3. Armed defence
4. Fighting
5. Threatening
6. Manipulating

7. Negotiating
8. Doing business
9. Exchanging
10. Working together
11. Helping where necessary
12. Courteous behaviour

Figure 4.3   There are different ways of working together

Travelling in a clockwise direction, the various axes show the following forms of human interaction:

- living without any real contact – avoiding the need to see others;

- snarling at one another;

- armed defence – not yet knowing if you need or can trust one another;

- fighting with one another – from name-calling to out-and-out war;

- threatening one another;

- manipulating one another;

- negotiating with one another – realising that we need each other, but realising that we are pursuing conflicting goals;

- doing business together;

- exchanging places, information and so on;

- working together – trusting one another and striving together towards the same or parallel goals, but never conflicting ones;

- helping one another if necessary;

- being courteous to one another.

Besides team behaviour, as described above, teams should consist of people with complementary competencies – in professional ability, in cognitive skills and in team behaviour. This complementarity is vital to the realisation of projects and programmes. Professional ability can be broken down into primary competencies in one or more areas that are necessary for carrying out the project or programme. Cognitive skills can be regarded as the ability to combine information, fantasies, experiences, ideas, opinions and decisions in such a way as to provide new possibilities for the team members, enabling them to pursue or achieve the goals or outcome of the project or programme effectively, efficiently, creatively and flexibly.

CREATING A PRODUCTIVE TEAM IS NOT EASY

If you are doing your job properly, the first thing you will do is to assess which professional skills and what type of team behaviour (creative, investigative, questioning) is necessary to bring your assignment to a successful conclusion. In an ideal world, team members are gathered together on the basis of this list of ideals. However, in the real world, teams are usually formed in a completely different way. Most people try and gather together as many of 'their kind of people' as they can ('their kind' in terms of professional ability, formal position in the organisation and style of cooperation), or alternatively anyone with time on their hands is assigned and expected to work enthusiastically!

Every team member should be expected to be committed to the task in hand, achieve the project deliverable or pursue the programme goals. If they do not feel at one with the task in hand, they cannot be expected to put in extra effort on its behalf. Conflicts are usually more easily solved when those concerned know what they hope to achieve by working together. When there is no commitment, individuals will tend to concentrate on personal or professional differences, because there is no reason to compromise or look at things from a different point of view. Commitment must be to the whole assignment and not just to a part of it. It is almost impossible to form a productive team when its members flit in and out at will. Each individual team member is jointly responsible for the commitment of the whole. The management of the permanent organisation must aim to ensure that the conditions are in place to facilitate this. However, all too often team members are taken away from their project or programme work because they are needed for other more urgent work.

Five team dysfunctions

The true measure of a team is that it accomplishes the task that it set out to achieve. To do this consistently, a team must overcome the so-called five dysfunctions of teams. According to Lencioni (2005) the first of these is *the absence of trust*. Members of successful teams trust one another at a fundamental, emotional level, and are comfortable enough with one another to show vulnerability, weaknesses, mistakes, fears and natural patterns of behaviour. Team members get to a point where they can be completely open with one another, holding nothing back.

The second dysfunction is *the fear of conflict*. Team members who trust one another are not afraid to engage in passionate dialogue around the issues and decisions that are key to the organisation's success. They do not hesitate to disagree with, challenge and question one another, all in the spirit of finding the best answers, discovering the truth and making sound decisions.

The third dysfunction is *lack of commitment*. Teams that engage in unfiltered conflict are able to achieve real agreement on important issues, even when various members of the team initially disagree. That is because they ensure that all opinions and ideas are put on the table and considered, giving confidence to team members that all options have been considered.

Dysfunction number four is *the avoidance of accountability*. Teams that commit to decisions and standards of performance do not hesitate to hold one another accountable for adhering to those decisions. What is more, they don't rely on the team manager as the primary source of accountability, they go directly to their peers.

The last dysfunction is *inattention to the task at hand*. Teams that trust one another, engage in conflict, commit to decisions, and hold one another accountable are very likely to set aside their individual needs and agendas and focus on what is best for the project or programme. They do not give in to the temptation to place their departments, career aspirations or egos ahead of the project or programme.

In the end, there must be a sense of mutual or team responsibility. It is not enough that one person holds responsibility for the completion of the assignment, the whole team must have a feeling of mutual responsibility. One important condition for achieving this is that those concerned must be allowed to manage the work process themselves and are given up-to-date accurate information of how their efforts are progressing. All too often, a team is made accountable for its deeds without first being given the tools necessary to carry out the task.

Teams need to recognise what stage of development they have reached

Despite the fact that teams can vary enormously, according to their composition, goals, previous history and limiting conditions, most teams develop in a more or less recognised pattern. Team members are faced with various problems during each phase of the team's development (see Figure 4.4). These problems will seldom be voiced but they can be inferred. The problems or questions we encounter are (Zenger et al. 1993):

*   *Forming* In this first phase team members want to know: 'What is expected from me?' and 'How do I fit in?' Anxiety quickly follows the initial excitement.

*   *Storming* Enthusiasm usually gives way to frustration and anger. There are jealousies, hostile subgroups and ground rules will splinter. People struggle to find ways to work together.

*   *Norming* The team gains its balance. People find standard ways to do their work. Team members hold back their good ideas for fear of further conflict.

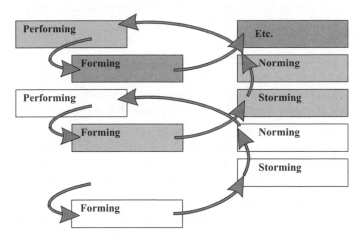

Figure 4.4   Stages in a team's development

- *Performing* In this fourth phase people have learned to disagree constructively and take measured risks, and apply their full energy to a variety of challenges. There is a high level of mutual trust. But the team can return to the forming phase when it adds or loses members or return to the storming phase when it goes through a stormy period.

YOU NEED TO RESPECT TEAM ROLES AND TO HANDLE CONFLICTS

Each member of the team has certain qualities and competencies, which we refer to as a team role. It is self-evident that each team role has its strengths and weaknesses. Belbin (1996) distinguishes the following team roles:

- The *coordinator* occupies themself with the selection of topics that require attention and with summarising and arranging discussions. They are often good at identifying someone's strong and weak points. Their qualities are a good sense of timing and balance and an ability to make others enthusiastic. They do not usually have any striking intellectual or creative capacities.

- The *shaper* looks for patterns in discussions, gives form to efforts and also steers towards agreement. They are enthusiasts and are confident in their ability. In discussions they soon identify the right patterns. They are downright intolerant of vague ideas.

- The *plant (inventor)* is especially good at generating new ideas, looking for solutions and likes to make to the point and critical remarks. Their tendency towards impracticality is compensated by their powers of imagination and independence of other people's opinions.

- The *monitor/evaluator* enjoys clarifying anything that is not clear and evaluating all kinds of suggestions in order to reach decisions. When doing this they usually make a good evaluation of other people's contributions.

Conflict situations are those situations in which the concerns of two people appear to be incompatible.

They can think critically and have the ability to reduce complexity. They have a built-in immunity from being overly enthusiastic. On the other hand, they do tend to be critical.

- The *implementer* converts ideas into something practical. They weigh up what can and cannot be used and carry out agreements in a systematic way. Their sense of realism, self-control and discipline counterbalance their tendency to shut themselves off from ideas that seem vague to them.

- The *(resource) investigator* look for ideas outside the group. To do this, they make and maintain contact with all sorts of people. They often introduce new ideas into the discussions. They are usually extrovert and thirst for knowledge but are less inclined to finish the job they are doing.

- The *teamworker* supports fellow team members, further develops the ideas of others and keeps the group process running smoothly. Teamworkers are the oil in the machine. They like people and are good listeners, but are not so good at making decisions.

- The *completer-finisher* is someone who stresses the need to finish things. In doing this, they exercise pressure on team members if necessary. They have an eye for detail and a great capacity to follow through. Their concern is order and efficiency. They are often loath to delegate, have self-control but are inclined to rush others.

- The *specialist* is a dedicated individual. Their priorities are maintaining professional standards and growing in their own field. Proud of their subject expertise, they tend to lack interest in others.

How to handle conflicts productively

Everyone experiences a conflict at one time or another. Even in the best of teams conflicts will arise now and again.

Conflicts can be useful, they can breathe a bit of life into a project or give a programme depth, but they can also be destructive, particularly for example if the conflict is really about nothing. Conflicts can be major with a great to-do, but also very small such as a simple difference of opinion during a meeting.

Conflicts can be about business (goals, problems, results and resources) or personal, where norms and identity are at issue. They can be long-standing and entrenched, or they may have only just begun.

Conflicts are perceived as negative: 'They take up a great deal of time and energy' or 'They spoil relationships and the atmosphere'. But conflicts can also have a positive side: they can clear the air and get things out into the open; and they can stimulate creative thinking to solve problems.

In conflict situations, we can describe a person's behaviour along two basic dimensions (*Thomas-Kilmann Conflict Mode Instrument* 1974). The first one, *assertiveness*, is the extent to which the individual attempts to satisfy their own concerns. The second one is called *cooperativeness*, the extent to which the individual attempts to satisfy the other person's concerns. These basic dimensions of behaviour can be used to define five specific methods of dealing with conflicts. These 'conflict-handling modes' are useful in some situations. Every mode represents a set of useful social skills. See Figure 4.5.

- *Competing* ('Might makes right') is assertive and uncooperative. It is a power-oriented mode. When competing you pursue your own concerns at the other person's expense. You use whatever power seems appropriate to win your position. You stand up for your rights, defend a position you believe is correct or simply try to win.

- *Accommodating* ('Kill your enemies with kindness') is unassertive and cooperative. It is the opposite of competing. You neglect your own concerns to satisfy the concerns of the other person. This mode contains an element of self-sacrifice. It might take the form of selfless generosity or charity. Sometimes you obey another person's order when you would prefer not to.

- *Avoiding* ('Leave well enough alone') is unassertive and uncooperative. You do not immediately pursue either your own concerns or those of the other person. You do not address the conflict. You simply withdraw from a threatening situation or you diplomatically sidestep an issue, postponing it until a better time.

- *Collaborating* ('Two head are better than one') is the opposite of avoiding. It is both assertive and cooperative. When you collaborate you attempt to work with the other person to find a solution that fully satisfies both concerns. You have to dig into an issue to identify the underlying concerns. Finally you have to find an alternative that meets both sets of concerns.

- *Compromising* ('Split the difference') is intermediate in both assertiveness and cooperativeness. You want to find an expedient, mutually acceptable solution that partially satisfies both parties. When you compromise you may split the difference, exchange concessions, or seek a quick middle-ground position.

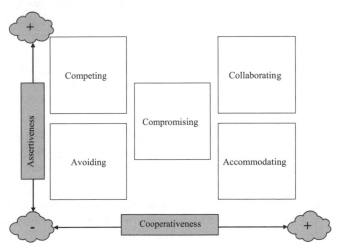

Figure 4.5   There are several alternatives for handling a conflict (Thomas-Kilmann)

Most people are capable of using all five conflict-handling modes. There is no single rigid style of dealing with conflict. But you may use some modes more readily than others and therefore tend to rely upon those modes more heavily. You use those conflict modes which are a result of both your personal predispositions and the requirements of the situations in which you find yourself; and your social skills may lead you to rely upon some conflict behaviours more or less than others.

EVERY NOW AND THEN PEOPLE NEED LEADERSHIP AND LEADERS NEED AUTHORITY

In projects and programmes, your tasks are often rather vague, and your authority may be equally unstated. To justify the responsibilities with which you are entrusted, you need the authority to assign work to your team members (within the framework of the project or programme plans). What is more, you must at least have the authority to take corrective action (within the margins of the plans).

You cannot lead without power

You cannot fulfil your obligation without having and using power in some form or other. The term 'power' often has unpleasant associations but it is really a neutral term. Power is sometimes described as 'the potential to influence behaviour, to change the course of events, to overcome resistance and to get people to do things that they would not do otherwise'.

Power or influence is inherent to all social systems and all human relationships. Power is therefore unavoidable and neutral; in itself, it is neither good nor bad. The 'power system' includes everyone, no one can escape it. However, one person's loss of power does not always mean more power for someone else.

Someone who can satisfy the needs of somebody else is potentially powerful. Power is often exercised by providing or withholding desired or necessary things from other people.

The more esteem a leader has as a person, the more power or influence they actually have over other people. At the same time, for the team to function well, team members should also feel empowered.

Every manager has some formal power, that is, the power that comes with your position, a source of authority awarded to you by the organisation. Your position as assignment leader enables you to do certain things. For example, you can impose penalties and give rewards such as the best work, an exciting business trip or a bonus. People will be willing to do things for you because they recognise the power that you are entitled to. On the basis of the position that you have been given, you will have access to all sorts of networks and data. The fact that you have been allocated resources such as people, equipment and money, means that you are in a position of power.

As distinct from positional power which is awarded by the organisation, there is the power that a person commands through their personality. This power is given to you by your team and may be referred to as charisma, influence, reputation, allure or authority. The team does things for you because they respect you, your knowledge, your experience or energy. In some cases, you get things done because people wish to be identified with you or want to be part of your assignment. The more others appreciate you, the more personal power will be attributed to you. And this positive recognition from others will grow as your qualities of openness, patience, willingness to accept the opinion of others, compassion, integrity, empathy and consistency increase.

Irrespective of the source of power, it is others who award it to you. If a team member is oblivious to any form of reward or penalty, they will not be concerned about the source of power. Team members can respond in a variety of ways to your authority. They can disregard it completely, they can be receptive and do what is asked of them and they can meekly agree to do what is asked because they think that it is the correct thing to do.

In order for the team to function well, it is important that its members feel that they too are empowered. The more autonomy they have, the more involved they will feel with the assignment. They need the feeling of being able to influence the course of events. You need to assume a less dominant role if you wish to empower your team members.

Persuation	Making a strong case for what you want while maintaining genuine respect for a subordinate's idea
Patience	Maintaining a long-term perspective in the face of short-term obstacles
Gentleness	Sensitivity in dealing with vulnerabilities subordinates may express
Teachable	Operating from the assumption than you do not know everything
Acceptance	Withholding judgement, giving the benefit of the doubt
Kindness	Remembering the little things (which are the big things) in relationships
Openness	Giving consideration to subordinates' intentions, values and desires rather than focusing exclusively on their behaviour
Compassionate	Acknowledging errors, mistakes and the need to make 'course corrections' in a context of genuine concern, making it safe to take risks
Consistency	Faced with crises or challenges: do not manipulate, but act according to your values, your personal code and character
Integrity	Honestly matching words and feelings with thoughts and actions

Figure 4.6   Ten attributes for acquiring power (Covey 1991)

Leadership involves getting things done for and by people

Leadership entails influencing the performance of others through personal contact. This process involves organising, coaching, motivating, instructing and delegating. The best style of leadership is one that is geared both to those who you are supervising and to the work they are carrying out. Team members usually enjoy working independently and this increases motivation.

But leadership is complicated: you need to combine elements that do not easily fit together. For example, you need to have good ideas and present them well, while seeking and listening to the ideas of others. You need to be able to build good relationships, even with those who do not trust you.

Decisive leaders attract many followers, but it is usually more a case of dependence than real involvement

Effective leaders are not those with the highest IQ, but those who combine mental intelligence with emotional intelligence (Goleman et al. 2002). Emotional intelligence involves the way you handle yourself and others. You need to be self-aware and self-controlled. You need to be able to read the political and social environment; to intuitively grasp what others want and need; what their strengths and weaknesses are; to remain healthy under stress; and to be able to develop a rapport with others.

Your leadership style should be adapted to different situations. When a team member is not competent for a given task (preparing a schedule or budgeting costs) or goes to pieces in times of crisis or repeated get-backs, a more instructing or authoritative style may be needed. When team members know what to do and how to do it, a more participative style is appropriate.

Remember, people perform different tasks, and for every task you have to know what you want them to accomplish. You have to pay attention to their readiness for this task, so you can use the appropriate leadership style; and give them what they need to be successful and effective.

Readiness of team members is a function of their *competence* to perform a task or function (knowledge, experience, skill) and their *willingness* (confidence, motivation, commitment). These two are interdependent: a change in one will change the other.

Situational leadership revolves around the idea that team members develop on a continuum between competence and willingness. An effective leader assesses a team member's developmental position and adapts their leadership style to match the team member's developmental level.

Of course there is a great deal more that determines your leadership efficiency: the role of significant peers, organisation culture, the expectations of other managers, decision time, job demands, demands from followers and your own personality. But according to Paul Hersey: 'This is too much for the day-to-day decision making. The most important variable is the relationship between leader and follower' (Hersey et al. 2000).

You need to match your leadership style to the competence and willingness of team members. When you try to influence others you will use *directive* (task) *behaviour* and *supportive* (relationship) *behaviour*. Directive behaviour means helping team members to achieve a goal by instructing them. This involves giving directions, agreeing goals (and giving instructions on how to achieve those goals, methods of evaluation and timelines, and defining roles. Supportive behaviour involves assisting team members, via a dialogue) to feel comfortable with themselves, their co-workers and the situation.

If you put all this together, you will see that there are four situational leadership styles (Hersey et al. 2000) or behaviours:

* *Instructing/telling* The leader focuses on task or goal achievement and spends less time using supportive behaviours: 'Do what I tell you.'
* *Persuading/selling* The leader focuses communication on both goal achievement and supporting subordinates. They explain, ask for suggestions and decide how the job will be done: 'What do you think?'
* *Supporting/coaching* The leader explains what is wanted, and supports the employee. The leader delegates day-to-day decision-making control, but is available to help with problem solving: 'I can give you support if you feel insecure.'
* *Delegating/democratic* The leader offers less task input and social support, but sets standards for the performance. They give team members control and refrain from intervention and unneeded social support: 'You have proven that you can and want to do the job; I'll be there if you need me.'

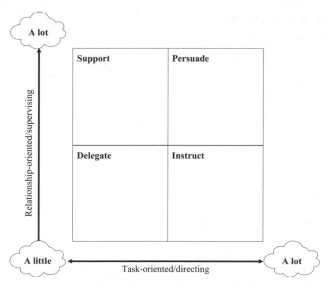

Figure 4.7   Appropriate styles of leadership

You cannot lead without trust

You need to develop the relationships between you and your team members (but also with other stakeholders). A healthy relationship needs trust. 'Trust is', in the words of the leadership guru Warren Bennis (1999), 'essential to all organisations.' The main determinant of trust is reliability, or consistency. It is knowing where someone is coming from, what they stand for. A recent study showed people would rather follow individuals they can count on, even when they disagree with their viewpoint, than people they agree with but who shift positions frequently.

Relational trust is forged in daily social exchanges – trust grows over time when you meet people's expectations. Relational trust erodes when people perceive that you are not acting in ways that are consistent with their understandings of your role. Relational trust includes competence, respect, personal regard for others and integrity. You need to know how to build the trust necessary for healthy relationships between all members and levels of the organisation(s).

There are three types of trust (Reina and Reina in Fullan 2001), all of which must be actively developed and reinforced:

* *Competence* trust (trust of capability):
    * respect people's knowledge, skills, and abilities;
    * respect people's judgement;
    * involve others and seek their input;
    * help people learn skills.
* *Contractual* trust (trust of character):
    * manage expectations;
    * establish boundaries;
    * delegate appropriately;
    * encourage a win-win attitude;
    * honour agreements;
    * be consistent.
* *Communication* trust (trust of disclosure):
    * share information;
    * tell the truth;
    * admit mistakes;
    * give and receive constructive feedback;
    * maintain confidentiality;
    * speak with good purpose.

And of course there is another leadership style: laissez faire or non leadership, that is, the absence of leadership. A hands-off let-things-ride approach, a leader who abdicates responsibility, delays decisions, gives no feedback and makes little effort to help subordinates satisfy their needs.

Effective leadership can be felt throughout a project or programme. It gives pace and energy to the work and empowers the workforce. Empowerment is the collective effect of leadership. In teams with effective leaders, empowerment is most evident in the way that people feel significant. Everyone feels that they are making a difference to the success of the project or programme.

CHAPTER 5

Helping Team Members Work Together – Checklists

In most cases a project or programme needs the involvement of a number of people to see it through. Working with, in or for a team is something that some people would rather avoid, despite the fact that working in teams is a regular topic of discussion. When it is not clear to everyone what the team should be or do, team members will be confused about what teamworking involves. You can't expect a team leader to provide all of the energy and guidance, on how to work as a team and what to do. Projects and programmes dealt with in this book can only be successfully completed if managed in a cooperative way!

Checklist 5.1

Create a Team

Teams vary enormously depending on their make up, goals, previous history and constraining factors. A team will develop according to a more or less recognised pattern. Team members will be faced with various problems during each stage of the team's development process. You need to deal with these issues at each stage, ignoring them won't help you or the team at all.

- ***How to build a productive team:***
  - Don't forget: the following stages are an integral part of a team development process:
    - *Forming* – team members look for acceptance. Help them to get to know and accept each other. Try to reach agreement on the purpose of the team and the ground rules for working together.
    - *Storming* – team members exchange information. There will be a lot of conflicts in this phase that you need to handle effectively if you are to avoid the team becoming frustrated or disillusioned.
    - *Norming* – integrating the team's goals. Your job is to help the team members to be open and frank, usually by increasing their responsibility and authority.
    - *Performing* – tackling and managing the interaction of the team. Step back and let the team demonstrate their capabilities.
  - Discuss problems and bottlenecks as soon as they become apparent:
    - make your dissatisfaction clear;
    - encourage and support others to do the same;
    - identify the problem;
    - take time to stop and think.
  - Concentrate on being accepted and encouraging the team to exchange information, achieve goal integration and manage interaction.

Notes

- Team development is a spiral movement that may go up as well as down.
- Developing a team is a never-ending task.
- A happy team is a high-performing team.

Checklist 5.2

Be Aware of Team Behaviour and Interaction

One of the most important characteristics of a team is that its members interact. People influence one another. Human behaviour can be divided into four categories:

- *Interactive behaviour* is cooperative, and involves working together and offering encouragement.
- *Defiant behaviour* involves opposition, criticism and withdrawal.
- *Dominant behaviour* implies leadership and staying above certain matters.
- *Subservient* behaviour is passive and involves following someone else's lead, being dependent on them.

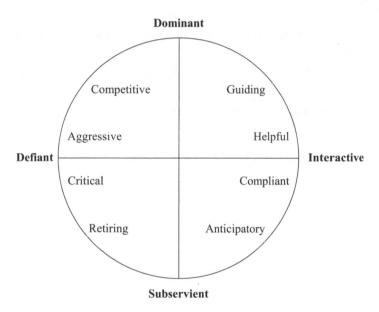

Figure 5.1   People influence each other in a variety of ways

- ***How to behave productively in your team:***
    - Bear in mind the way you behave will evoke a response in someone else:
        - interactive behaviour will encourage cooperation;
        - defiant behaviour will encourage others to oppose or marginalise you;
        - dominant behaviour will encourage people to follow your lead;
        - subservient will encourage colleagues to walk all over you.

- Try and influence someone showing defiant behaviour to adopt a more cooperative approach by behaving cooperatively yourself and avoiding confrontation.
- Bear in mind:
  - An effective team will manifest every type of behaviour. Defiant behaviour may sound negative, but a team must be able to be self-critical. It is self-evident that leaders must show dominant behaviour and followers must be more subservient.
  - Not all behaviour patterns are appropriate in certain situations; someone being obstructive is not effective if you are planning to climb a mountain together!
  - All behaviour patterns can degenerate into a caricature; submissiveness is no bad thing but slavish behaviour must be avoided!

Notes

- Supervision can degenerate into a take-over and helpfulness can become patronising.
- Criticism can often sound negative and personal, if not delivered with care.
- Aggressive behaviour is often destructive.

Checklist 5.3

Make Use of Team Members' Competencies

Each member of the team will have certain team role(s). Each of these team roles has its own strengths and weaknesses.

Try to ensure that you have a productive combination of team roles. You can start by helping team members to be aware of the roles they prefer to fill.

- *How to effectively use team member's competencies:*

  - Try to select team members to give you a complete set of team roles, overlapping the roles where necessary.
  - Make use of people's strengths in their chosen role.
  - Encourage team members to behave naturally.
  - Recognise respect and make use of the differences in how team members behave and encourage everyone to do the same.

Notes

- Everyone has their own preferred team role(s).
- Each project phase or programme stage requires a team with a specific mix of talents.
- People can fill more than one role.

You can lead a horse to water, but you can't make it drink.

Checklist 5.4

Work Together

Content, procedures and interaction are the three equally important elements of working together in groups or teams on projects and programmes.

To be able to work together, you must first want to.

- *How to enable your team to work together:*

  - Discuss the content (exchange information; define what must be achieved and what not).

  - Pay attention to the procedures (how the team is formally organised; rules for meetings and agendas; ways of reporting).

  - Look at the interaction (encourage team members to express themselves and to listen openly to one another; help them handle tension, conflict or disagreement).

Notes

- Content and procedure can be planned beforehand. However, you can't plan interaction. How people interact only becomes apparent when they start to do so.

- This does not mean that you can't manage the progress of interaction.

- Poor interaction within the team has a negative effect on both the content and the procedure.

Checklist 5.5

Make Careful Decisions

When someone is confronted with a problem, their first reaction is to jump straight to a solution. In so doing, they run the risk of being blind to any alternative solutions.

An even greater danger could be that by reverting to problem-solving behaviour, they could find a solution for the wrong problem! Every decision may be seen as a problem to be solved; but an effective decision-making process consists of a number of steps.

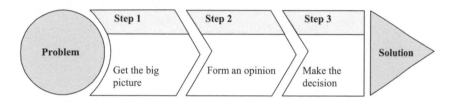

| Problem | Step 1 | Step 2 | Step 3 | Solution |

Get the big picture → Form an opinion → Make the decision

Figure 5.2   A sound decision is understood and accepted by all those concerned

- *How to make the right decisions:*

  - Step 1: concentrate on getting the big picture:
    - Describe the purpose of the decision in broad terms.
    - Gather and exchange all available information (facts, feelings and opinions).
    - Agree upon the decision-making process.
    - Monitor this process.
    - Don't even try and think of a solution yet!

  - Step 2: form an opinion:
    - Explore the various opinions about the information available.
    - Formulate the requirements that a solution must meet.
    - List everyone's views about the possible solutions.
    - Ask everyone's opinion and ensure that the interaction process is running smoothly.
    - Don't even try to pick the best solution yet!

  - Step 3: make the decision:
    - Choose which solution to adopt based on the team's agreement.
    - Review the possible consequences and decide if these are acceptable.

Decision making is not jumping to conclusions.

- Agree how to implement the decision.
- Monitor the interaction process, do not overrule or ignore anyone.
- Make the decision.

Notes

- A vague agreement that everyone assents to is not a decision.
- A decision not to decide for the time being, is also a decision.
- The team's decisions can be influenced by 'group think'.

Checklist 5.6

Consult Effectively

Consultation is vitally important if a team is to function successfully. Informal, bilateral consultation is often adequate, but you will also need to consult the whole team on a regular basis.

Try and reach agreement on how and when you will consult the team – perhaps at a weekly team meeting.

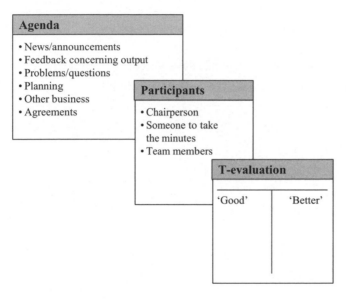

Agenda
- News/announcements
- Feedback concerning output
- Problems/questions
- Planning
- Other business
- Agreements

Participants
- Chairperson
- Someone to take the minutes
- Team members

T-evaluation

'Good'	'Better'

Talk doesn't get the work done.

Figure 5.3   Some tools for effective consultation

- ***How to consult effectively:***

    - Make sure you have a competent chairperson, someone who can:
        - prepare an adequate agenda and ensure that items on the agenda are dealt with according to procedure;
        - ensure that everyone has their say;
        - manage time;
        - wrap-up the discussion points;
        - summarise discussions and draw conclusions.

    - Check that people know how to behave in meetings. An effective participant will raise points that they consider important, listen to others and remain involved.

    - Make sure that the agenda covers the ground but is manageable. Where possible it should contain items that:
        - all the participants are aware of before the meeting starts;

- – are agreed to by all those present;
- – can be amended by the participants.
- • If possible, carry out a T-evaluation at the end of *each* session. This kind of evaluation:
  - – encourages team members to give feedback;
  - – highlights what went well and what could have been better.
- • List the points agreed during the meeting; limit this list to actions and agreements.

Notes

- • It is better to deal with a small number of points thoroughly than with a large number inadequately.
- • Real consultation involves all those who have a point to make.
- • Consultation is not necessarily decision making.

Checklist 5.7

Manage Conflicts

Conflicts do not always have to be resolved, but every conflict must be handled.

Even in the best of teams conflicts will arise now and again. They can be useful, but they can also be destructive.

Conflicts can be about goals, results and resources or about people's behaviour and the team's identity. Conflict can be helpful or damaging.

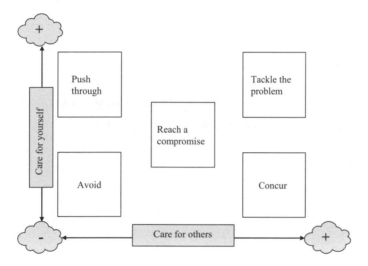

Figure 5.4   Conflicts can be handled in various ways

- *How to handle conflicts constructively:*

  - Push through when:
    - quick, decisive action is vital;
    - unpopular courses of action need to be implemented for important issues.
  - Tackle the problem when:
    - an integrated solution needs to be found and the concerns of both parties are too important to be compromised;
    - you need to gain commitment by incorporating the concerns of others into a consensual decision.
  - Compromise when:
    - two opponents with equal power are strongly committed to mutually exclusive goals;
    - you need a temporary settlement of complex issues.

- Avoid when:
  - an issue is trivial or more important issues are pressing;
  - you have little influence (you can see no chance of satisfying your concerns).
- Concur when:
  - you realise that you are wrong;
  - you want to build up social credit for later issues.

Notes

- Try to determine the root cause of the conflict.
- When you think you know the issues, summarize your understanding of them and ask if your summary accurately describes the other person's concerns.
- Work out the difference collaboratively wherever possible.
- No single approach is going to be universally effective.

Checklist 5.8

Listen and Question Effectively

Every form of cooperation involves communication.

Communication requires two basic skills: the ability to listen and the ability to ask questions.

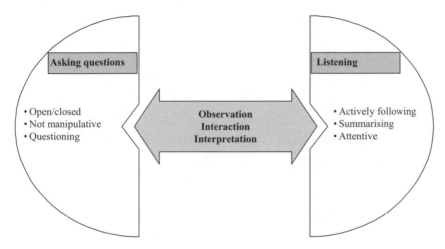

Figure 5.5   Questioning and listening are essential for communicating

*   ***How to question and listen effectively:***

    *   Listen actively:

        –   Show someone you are listening to them by giving short verbal cues or by nodding your head.

        –   Demonstrate you are listening actively by occasionally summarising what the other person has said.

        –   Remain attentive and allow them to correct your interpretation.

    *   Listen attentively: avoid formulating an answer while the other person is still talking.

    *   Keep an open mind.

    *   Ask open questions. Questions such as ' What do you think?', will get you the most information. More specific information can be gathered by asking a closed question, such as 'Have you started the report?'

    *   Leading questions can undermine the reliability of information you will be given. ('I'm sure you agree that…' or 'I'm sure you're glad that…').

    *   Continue to ask questions; they are often the only way to get to the bottom of something. Do not be satisfied with a short answer, but get to know the who, the whys and the wherefores.

Your view of the truth is not necessarily the same as anyone else's.

Notes

- Silence can also express an opinion.
- Leading questions elicit unreliable answers.
- Do not underestimate the power of non-verbal communication.

Checklist 5.9

Give and Receive Feedback

You cannot learn anything from one another without feedback. We can only improve if other people let us know what went well and where there is room for improvement. Without necessarily being aware of it, we give each other feedback in the way we respond to others people's behaviour. What you say lets the other person know what you think of them or their ideas.

What you don't know does the most damage.

Conscious feedback involves giving information to someone about how you perceive, understand or experience their behaviour and how you respond to it. This kind of feedback also expresses an opinion about performance. Everyone values honest opinions, personal appreciation and constructive criticism.

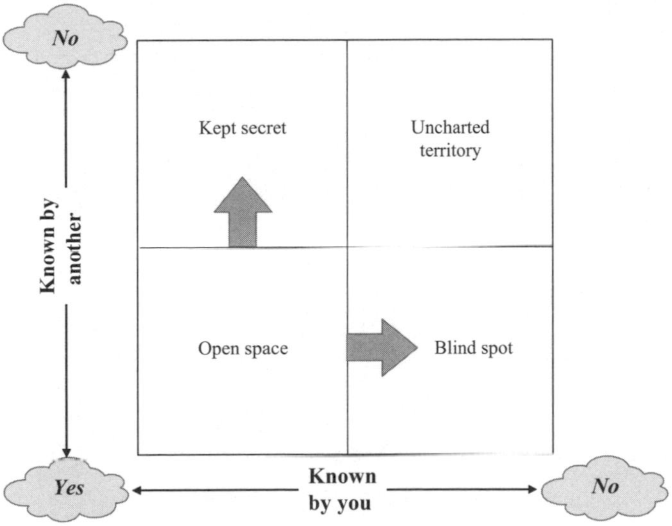

Figure 5.6   Without feedback you can't know yourself

- *How to handle feedback:*

    - Focus on behaviour that can be changed.
    - Do not speak for others, speak only for yourself.
    - Be specific, do not generalise.
    - Describe what you have observed, do not be judgmental.
    - Link the feedback to actual situations.
    - Describe what effect this behaviour has on you.
    - Be aware of what effect your feedback is having on the other person.
    - When receiving feedback:

- listen attentively and ask questions to seek further information;
- try not to deny, defend or explain;
- investigate how you can best use the feedback;
- remember that you can always ask for feedback.

Notes

- Being given feedback is not always easy; accepting it is even harder.
- People receiving feedback often take it personally, regarding it as personal criticism and that the person giving the feedback does not like them.
- Remember the basic rules of feedback: you are free to accept, question or reject any feedback you are given.

Checklist 5.10

Acquire Power and Authority

Power is defined as the ability to induce a person to do something they would not otherwise have done.

Power is a resource that may or may not be used.

Power can but should not be misused.

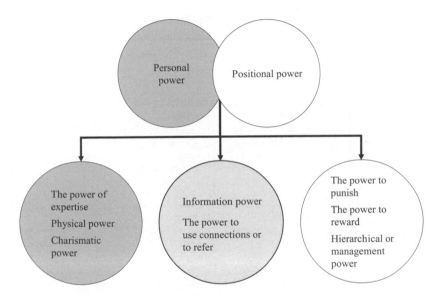

Personal power

Positional power

The power of expertise

Physical power

Charismatic power

Information power

The power to use connections or to refer

The power to punish

The power to reward

Hierarchical or management power

Figure 5.7   You have a number of sources of power

- *How to obtain sufficient power:*
    - Make sure you have a voice in determining resources (jobs, money, tools and so on).
    - Gather information about relevant processes, products and services.
    - Get to know important people, bodies and parties.
    - Ensure that people want to identify with you personally or with your ideas.
    - Ensure that other people believe that they depend on you.

Notes

- Fear is a motive for not doing something.
- Someone who checks everything sees nothing.
- Showing trust engenders trust.

Checklist 5.11

Choose Your Style of Leadership

Leadership involves influencing the performance of others through personal contact. It uses skills such as organising, coaching, motivating, instructing and delegating. The best style of leadership is geared to those who you are supervising and the work they are carrying out.

Team members usually enjoy working independently. Independent working increases motivation and allows the manager more scope to deal with other matters.

A lot

Relation-oriented supervising

Support:	Persuade:
• determine the what and how together	• discuss the what and how together
• assist during the implementation	• monitor the implementation
Delegate:	**Instruct:**
• leave the what and how	• tell the what and how
• assist during the implementation	• check the implementation
• use personal power	• use positional power

A little ← Task-oriented directing → **A lot**

Competent willing	Competent unwilling	Incompetent willing	Incompetent unwilling

Figure 5.8   A project or programme manager needs to choose an appropriate style of leadership

• ***How to determine the right leadership style:***

   • *Instruct* if the team member is less competent but motivated. Give precise written instructions and carefully control their implementation.

   • *Persuade* if the team member is moderately competent. Offer clear guidance and give emotional support if necessary.

   • *Support* if the team member is competent but not very secure. Offer minimum guidance and more coaching.

   • *Delegate* if the team member is competent as well as motivated. Delegate as much work as you can; create conditions for a motivated team.

Notes

- Encourage your team members to take their jobs seriously.
- Gradually reduce the amount of supervision and accept the increased risk.
- Be quick to offer positive feedback when performance improves.

CHAPTER 6

Managing Your Project – The Approach

A project is a unique result or deliverable that has been personally agreed and that must be realised with limited means and through a unique complex of activities. It is an artificial concept. Managers adopt a specific series of unique and temporary, result-oriented activities (that have to be completed with limited resources) and call it a 'project'.

A project consists of a number of phasing (non-managerial, content activities), managing (planning and control activities) and decision-making activities or processes. These will be carried out with limited means to reach a unique deliverable. Not everything that is called a project is actually a project or should be tackled as such. A project management methodology is only appropriate when a project meets certain preconditions.

You need to ensure that a project has an adequate number of the characteristics found in the ideal project, before considering a project methodology. These characteristics are:

- a defined beginning and end;
- oriented towards a deliverable, result or product;
- unique;
- multidisciplined;
- complicated;
- uncertain;
- costly;
- essential to those concerned;
- can be controlled from one point;
- has a single owner, principal or client.

Once you have decided that you will carry out a certain assignment as a project, using the project management methodology, you need to recognise the consequences. You need to accept that you can and will work in a project-oriented way. This chapter is about the *method*: the language, the rules of the game and how to start and manage a project. Of course, the methods for project management (phasing, managing and decision making, see Figure

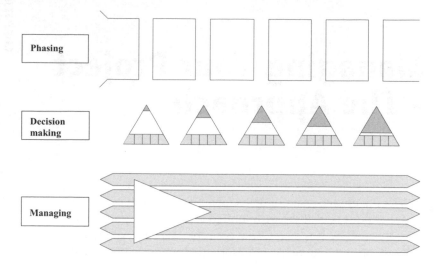

Figure 6.1   The project management method integrates phasing, managing and decision making

6.1) cannot and must not be seen as being separate from the other project management processes of organising and team building.

There are 12 rules for professional project management:

1. Those involved in a project recognise that routine tasks need to be managed differently from special or one-off assignments. This means you need agreement on the goals, deliverable and approach of each project.
2. There is a division of labour between the responsibility for the formulation of the project goals and for the expected result or deliverable (the first is the responsibility of the owner while the second rests with the project manager).
3. Those involved can use the project to pursue alternative goals, as long as the deliverable they want to achieve through the project is a shared one.
4. There is only one appointed owner. Someone who must be capable of taking on key decisions during the project. The owner ensures that project management and decision making are substantially speeded-up and simplified.
5. The owner needs to define the goals of the project; the desired result/ product/deliverable before anything can start. They also need to ensure that the requisite means (people, investment, materials) are in place.
6. The task of ensuring that the right things are done is the responsibility of the owner. The project manager's task is to make sure they are done correctly.
7. The project owner and project manager should involve the project team members as early as possible; the sooner they are involved, the more committed they will be to the implementation of the project.
8. Users, support staff and administrators need to be involved in the project at an early stage.
9. The project manager and owner ensure that the assignment meets the characteristics of a project (unique, uncertain, important to those involved,

clear goals, result-oriented).

10. The project should be managed by focussing on four components: the key players, environment, interaction and method.

11. Before the project manager can get down to work, they will ensure the project decision document has been agreed. In this document the project deliverable is defined as well as the phasing activities to be carried out and the project management plans.

12. The owner should be willing to take the decision at the end of each phase whether or not to continue the project.

Over the past decades, more and more managers have come to recognise that project management is an effective and efficient method for implementing special assignments. Unfortunately, many of those who try to manage projects often do so in an unconsciously fragmented and uninformed way.

The following pages are about the vocabulary and the basics of the project management method. The other building blocks of project management are dealt with in the chapters on organising and team building. Our project management method is based on our experience of some thirty years consulting on and managing projects in a variety of contexts such as organisation renewal and improvement; research and development; housing, building and construction; policy formulation and implementation; and the development and implementation of information systems. These projects all differ one from another but, their management has many things in common. Our project management method can be applied to internal projects, product development, change management and so on, and external projects such as supplying systems, implementing mergers, building offices and roads, all of which involve external owners.

The 12 common characteristics of our project management methodology are:

1. thinking and acting with the deliverable in mind (the end product);

2. thinking first (from broad outlines to finer details), then acting;

3. making a distinction between non-managerial or content activities and managerial ones (managing time, money, quality, release and organisation);

4. a systematic approach to the initiation, realisation and hand over of a project;

5. making an inventory of all non-managerial activities and a sequence (phases) in which these activities are to be carried out;

6. drawing up plans and seeking approval for the five project management perspectives of time, money, quality, release and organisation (taking into account the risks associated with the margins of each of these) and an ongoing process of 'check and improve';

7. opting to stop or continue the project, keeping also in mind the project start document (the project brief or the business case);

8. integrating the outcome of the previous phase of a project with the forecast of the non-managerial activities that need to be implemented in the subsequent phase or phases and, if necessary, adjusting the plans for the

five project management perspectives in a decision document;
9. the clear delegation of tasks, responsibilities and powers;
10. controlled management of changes to the decision documents;
11. involving interested parties at the right time and on the right issues;
12. taking decisions (based upon a decision document) at the end of each phase.

WHAT IT'S ALL ABOUT: GOALS AND A DELIVERABLE

For a project to succeed, it is essential that all the parties that participate in one way or another want to achieve the same deliverable. Other words to describe what is meant by 'deliverable' are result, product, service, solution or output.

A project deliverable should be a specific tangible or intangible object; one that is achievable and feasible and can be verified by the project owner.

One of the first project activities involves clarification of the issues, problems or goals in order to arrive at a clear description of the project deliverable (see Figure 6.2). This process requires empathy from the project manager and openness on the part of the project owner (also called the sponsor, client, principal or user). The project owner should be someone who wants to solve a problem or who sees an opportunity that cannot be passed up. Good owners experience both the joys and the sorrows of a project. They are the people who can anticipate the consequences of different choices and who are going to make use of the deliverable (see Chapter 2).

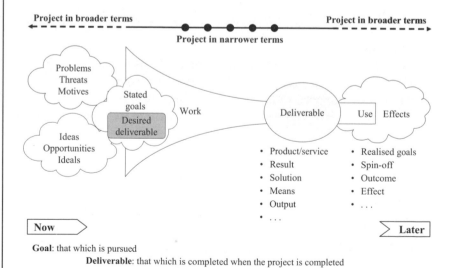

Goal: that which is pursued
Deliverable: that which is completed when the project is completed
Work: that which must be done to make the project deliverable

Figure 6.2   A project is oriented towards goals or problems, but above all towards one deliverable

The project owner must be willing to make information about the assignment available. They must also be prepared to state their own goals, aspirations and ambitions. Some owners are uncomfortable with this approach and feel that project managers should just do as they are told. Projects require extra effort from project managers. They too should be able to commit themselves to the project, to believe in it and to feel it is feasible.

By examining the context in which the project is to be realised, the project manager gains insight into the various forces surrounding the assignment. A project's feasibility depends on two aspects: technical (is the necessary know-how present and available?) and social (will those involved such as staff members, line managers and society at large allow the result to be produced and used?).

PHASING THE PROJECT

The description of the project deliverable is the basis for an inventory of the content or phase *activities* that need to be carried out in a logical sequence. You need to identify the activities to run between the start and completion of the project. No matter how you look at it, there are always at least three phases: starting up, realising/implementing and using/maintaining (see Figure 6.3).

The phasing details vary from one project methodology to another. Some methods adapt the phases to fit in with the management cycle of the client organisation. If the project owner and the steering committee or management team meet to discuss the project once a quarter, a phase will be defined to reflect this quarterly time period. This is sometimes referred to as a 'management phase': the period within which the project manager is empowered to carry out the project.

In complex projects, in addition to making an inventory of activities it is also important to group tasks into phases. Each and every one of the activities must be assigned to a particular phase (see Figure 6.4). As we shall see later, phasing is necessary for planning and controlling the progress of the actual project.

Starting up **Realising** **Using**

Figure 6.3 The three basic phases of a project

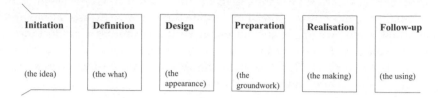

Initiation	Definition	Design	Preparation	Realisation	Follow-up
(the idea)	(the what)	(the appearance)	(the groundwork)	(the making)	(the using)

Figure 6.4   Phases of a project

Phasing a project helps you structure your decision making and it reduces uncertainty because it makes progress visible. Phasing involves grouping related activities together. Each phase must be treated equally, not necessarily in terms of time or required resources but definitely in terms of importance. The transition between each phase is a logical point for the owner to make the decision either to continue or discontinue the project.

Dividing a project into six phases will reduce even the most complex projects to activities and tasks that can be planned and executed with confidence.

The *initiation phase* of a project is the only phase that does not have a clearly defined beginning. By the end of this phase, the project deliverable must be known and the way in which this deliverable is to be achieved must be determined (whether via a project methodology or in some other way).

The *definitions phase* is the phase in which the project deliverable is specified (for a project with a tangible outcome) in terms of external interfaces, functional and operational requirements and design constraints (see Chapter 8). This phase provides the answer to the question, 'What will the result do or perform?'

Project deliverables requirements are sometimes classified in other ways. In the case of a softer project, such as the development of a new policy, the following classification of requirements is made:

- Effect requirements: what are the desired effects of the successful project and what prerequisites does it have? Examples are an effective decision-making process in the management board on the policy described in a memo, clear support in the determination of a point of view, transparent information on the results of a choice.

- Content requirements: what should be the content? For instance the requirements clearly indicate what decisions are to be taken, the topics that have to be dealt with and the depth in which they are to be discussed.

- Design requirements: what do the requirements of the successful project imply for the design of the policy document or the memo? For instance, a standard layout, no longer than 25 pages, with clear diagrams and graphs may be required.

In the *design phase*, the project begins to take concrete form as the chosen solutions, those that will meet the project requirements, are described. The design phase provides the answer to the question: 'What should the result look like?'

In the *preparation phase*, everything required during the actual realisation of the project is made ready and available. Organisational and technical designs are prepared including production plans, training programs, task instructions and so on. Time spent during this phase will help you to ensure that the implementation can take place smoothly 'by just pressing a button'.

In the *realisation phase* the project is finally implemented: for example, the organisation change process is carried out or the new IT system is built along the lines of the project requirements.

In the *follow-up phase* the result of the project is used, kept, maintained and, if necessary, modified. The content activities in this phase include using, supporting and maintaining the realised deliverable, and supporting and maintaining the tools, aids and resources associated with it. This phase is not part of the project as such and the project team is responsible for planning but not carrying it out. The owner of the project is the person responsible for making sure the follow-up phase happens.

Figure 6.5 summarises the purpose of each phase of a project.

MANAGING THE PROJECT

Planning and progress control of a project are continuous activities. Phasing the project helps you to find out what activities have to be done, and to do

Phase	Purpose
Initiation	Consider what the project deliverable or result should and should not be; all those involved have the same picture
Definition	Consider exactly what the project deliverable should do (external interfaces, functional and performance requirements, design constraints)
Design	Consider what the project deliverable should look like
Preparation	Consider what the project deliverable should look like, once made. By 'pressing a button' the required project deliverable will appear
Realisation	The carrying out or implementation of the project deliverable: making it tangible
Follow-up	Using, supporting, maintaining and dismantling the project deliverable

Figure 6.5   Each phase of a project has a specific purpose

them. Managing the project will enable you to ensure that it will be executed according to plan. There are five management perspectives that need to be addressed. These perspectives are project time management (abbreviated to time), project money management (abbreviated to money), project quality management (abbreviated to quality), project release management (abbreviated to release) and project organisation management (abbreviated to organisation).

For each of the five perspectives it needs to be clear:

*   what is the management requirement (norm, standard , plan) with margins (or contingencies);
*   who is responsible for progress control and how often will it be done;
*   how should data be processed into a progress report ;
*   who is authorised to adjust the management plans (within and outside the set margins).

Project time management Have the beginning and end dates of the project been set and have the related number of man-hours, materials and other resources been determined? This will involve: estimating the total lead-time and the lead-time for each activity and relating each activity to dates in the calendar. Once you have done this, you need to allocate the required human and other resources for each activity. This involves seeking approval for and issuing schedules to all concerned.

Project money management Is there a budget that makes it clear what the limits of the project cost are and what the expected returns should be?

Money management involves: estimating the total expenditures and revenues for the project; detailing the costs for each activity to be carried out; relating all expected expenditures and revenues to dates in the calendar; obtaining approval of all your preliminary calculations, cash flow, estimates and budget schedules; and issuing the approved schedules and budgets to all concerned.

Project quality management Is it clear how good the result must be and how this is to be demonstrated? Quality management in a project involves ensuring that the project conforms to agreed quality requirements, by providing controllable, measurable criteria, and conducting defined quality control tests. How closely does the project deliverable meet the quality requirements (good is good enough)?

Important quality management tasks include: specifying quality requirements for the project outcome and ensuring that all these requirements can and will be controlled appropriately.

Project release management Are there any procedures for drawing up, releasing, changing and distributing decision documents?

This involves: identifying what information needs to be managed; deciding on a decision-document coding system; determining who must release each decision document; determining who must receive each decision document; via whom the documents will be transmitted; and in what form, where, and by whom each decision document will be filed and can be changed.

Project organisation management Have you established all the relevant organisational structures, such as project ownership, project management, project team composition, division of tasks, responsibilities, authority and lines of communication? Does everybody know how various decisions are to be made?

Important organisation management tasks include: ensuring that tasks, responsibilities and authority are unambiguously assigned; defining the formal channels of communication such as meetings; setting up both formal and informal decision-making processes; getting groups and individuals within the project to function operationally; setting up formal networks for communication and relationship management between the project organisation and its environment.

Figure 6.6 summarises the purpose of each management perspective.

The management of these five perspectives need to be in tune with each other. For example, it would be inappropriate to spend a great deal of energy on time if you neglect quality control. At the same time, adding additional funds to a project will not necessarily decrease lead-times or improve its quality.

DECISION MAKING

Throughout a project life you need to take decisions and make choices. There are various levels of decision making. For example, a decision must be

Management perspective	Purpose
Time	Ensuring that the project deliverable/result is realised on time (within the set margins) and that the content project activities are carried out by the people and means delegated in the time allotted
Money	Ensuring that the project is profitable (within the set margins), that the costs do not exceed the budget and that the planned revenues of the project deliverable can be achieved
Quality	Ensuring that the project deliverable is good enough, i.e. that it conforms to the quality requirements (within the set margins), that interim deliverables are tested against the quality requirements and that the necessary resources for testing are available
Release	Ensuring that the project deliverable is unequivocally recorded and approved (within the set margins); which of the decision documents is valid, who is party to the information in these documents and in which way they may be changed
Organisation	Ensuring that the project deliverable can be handed over to the owner and that everyone knows the tasks, responsibilities and authority (within the set margins) of all those involved, as well as what cooperation, communication and jobs will need to be carried out to achieve the project deliverable

Figure 6.6   Different purposes of each management perspective

made as to whether to start the project and what priority the project should have. Senior management usually makes such external decisions; they are responsible for the long-term development of the organisation and can therefore judge whether and how a project fits into this picture.

Then there are the large number of decisions that are made during each phase, such as who to interview, what measurement technique to use or how to keep those involved informed. Decisions such as these are made by the project manager and the project team members.

In our approach to project management, the most important decisions are those that are made at the end of each phase, as to whether or not to continue the project. The project owner (possibly in consultation with senior management and the stakeholders) is responsible for these decisions.

To help them make these decisions systematically, they have access to decision (or baseline) documents. These documents will include the contracts, tenders, plans, proposals, task descriptions, milestones, offers, consolidation documents and agreements associated with the project.

In making decisions at the transition of one phase to the next, you need to avoid reversing earlier decisions. At the same time, these decisions should not unnecessarily hinder the project's remaining life cycle. The nature of the decisions the project owner needs to make is, therefore, linked to the phase of the project (see Figure 6.7).

Decision documents enable you to integrate and record the results of the previous phase or phases. The documents also specify what needs to be done in the next phase(s), how much time and what resources this will take, what the financial consequences will be, how the quality of the project deliverable will be assured, released and adjusted and what everyone's tasks, responsibilities and authority are. In this sense, the decision document looks ahead. As soon as the project owner has approved the decision document's contents, it becomes a contract – the basis for the subsequent phases.

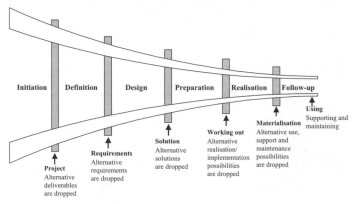

Figure 6.7   Decisions to be made in a project

Hence, a decision document is not just the *conclusion* of a previous phase, it is also the *starting point* for the next one. This document, provides the project manager with a contract from the project owner that defines the deliverable to be achieved, the work necessary to achieve it and the management plans of the relevant perspectives. Decisions that are needed during the phase or phases that fall within the set margins of this contract can be made by the project manager personally.

The project owner must be notified immediately about any imminent deviations from the contract.

In order to ensure consistency, the decision documents must all be structured in the same way and include:

- A description of the project deliverable, as far as this can be deduced on the basis of the activities of that phase of the project.
- A description of the work to be carried out. Each of the work activities should be described in detail for the subsequent phase and more generally for the later phases.
- A description of the management plans (covering time, money, quality, release and organisation) and the set-up for progress reporting (who controls progress, how and how often, and who adjusts and re-plans what, and how?).

A decision document also works as an important means of communication. The regular exchange of ideas at the end of each phase allows ideas about the project, and associated expectations as to what will and what will not be realised, to be brought into line. This also ensures that it isn't just the project team members who are engaged in the project; other stakeholders are involved too.

One way to ensure that the project owner stays committed and continues to feel responsible is to regularly inform them about the project's progress. At the very least, this should be done during the transition from one phase to the next. This will enable the project owner to reinforce their responsibility for the project since they have a tool at their disposal, namely, the decision documents.

Professional project management saves all those involved a great deal of inconvenience. But this does not mean a project runs itself. A project always requires a temporary combination of human resources and this demands extra time and energy from all involved.

Every project involves a commitment of time, attention and resources from the project owner, the project manager and the project team. This means that an organisation will only ever be able to implement a limited number of projects at any one time.

Professional project management can help to start or initiate (see Chapter 7) and to execute or complete (see Chapter 8) your project, which is a unique, costly and complex assignment, one that involves many complex tasks and deadlines and regular communication across organisational boundaries. Working on a project will be a learning experience for all those involved.

Initiating/Starting Your Project – Checklists

In many cases a project involves a number of people and often includes team members from other departments or organisations. This can make the specification of your project difficult and time consuming. All these people have their own different language for (and experience of) projects. But your project must mean the same thing to all those concerned.

In order to specify your project you need to specify the 'why' (problems and goals) and the 'what' (deliverable or result) of your project (see Figure 7.1).

The next activity is to make a plan. The specification of the deliverable is the basis of a good project path or plan. Thirdly you have to prepare the five management plans for the five management perspectives of time, money, quality, release and organisation (including the progress control procedures). Finally you must integrate the outcome of all these activities in the *project brief;* the first decision document.

Be careful not to fudge the issue by accepting conflicting demands or contradicting requirements in the hope that it will all turn out right in the end.

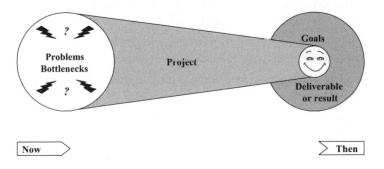

Figure 7.1   The project helps you to get from now (strategy and problems) to then (deliverable and goals)

Checklist 7.1

Define The What and The Why of Your Project

Every project starts with a description of the goals to be pursued or the problems to be solved and a definition of what you need to produce or realise. This last point, the project deliverable, must be determined beforehand. As long as you have not defined it with sufficient clarity, carrying out any kind of phasing or content activities becomes a very risky business.

- ***How to prepare a proper specification of the why and what:***

  - Determine (1) the intentions, (2) the expectations and (3) the opinions of all those involved in the project.

  - List those parts of the intentions, the expectations and the opinions that can be achieved and the possible consequences if they are not achieved.

  - Describe any current problems and bottlenecks (or those expected in the near future) and, where possible, back these up with facts and figures.

  - List those parts of the problems or bottlenecks that can be solved and the possible consequences if you don't achieve these objectives.

  - Give an unambiguous description of the project's deliverable or end result. A project deliverable is what has been achieved when the project is finished. The project deliverable can be a product, an output, a system, an agreement, a research report, a book and so on. The project deliverable may be tangible as well as intangible.

  - Make it clear what does not belong within the project deliverable (that is, what are the project boundaries).

  - Investigate the basic feasibility and of all the critical elements of the deliverable.

  - Ensure that everyone involved understands the importance of the project.

Notes

- The project deliverable should not be formulated as a goal or intended effect; for example a cleaner train, better trained people.

- Make sure the description of the project deliverable is not too vague; for example 'the most effective form of intranet'.

- Make sure you have also defined what the deliverable is not (as well as what it is).

Checklist 7.2

Define The Work That Needs Doing

A good specification of the deliverable or result is the basis of a good project path or plan. The project path is always most detailed for the phase about to be started and more general for later phases.

Only when the deliverable has been adequately determined and defined, can you turn your thoughts to the actual phase activities that need to be implemented. These are the activities that enable you to achieve this deliverable. They should be laid down in the sequence in which they should be carried out in a project plan or project decision document. However, your project plan should not be a straitjacket. It is based on what you know now – the situation as it now stands – and should only give an indication of how best the project can be carried out. A project plan is always more detailed for today than tomorrow. Insights and circumstances change constantly and so must your plan, but always in a controlled way and never implicitly.

- *How to prepare a proper project plan:*
  - Draw up the project plan by describing the non-managerial activities in each phase in the correct order.
  - Start with a detailed description of the definition phase; where necessary describing how these activities will be tackled.
  - Follow up with a more general description for the remaining phases.
  - Consider the activities in sequence from beginning to end, but double check your plan by working backwards from the end to the beginning too.
  - Go through the planning process with those who will actually be carrying out the work.
  - Agree the natural/logical order for carrying out the activities.
  - Identity which activities could be carried out simultaneously (you may need to split some of them up).
  - Make sure that the description of each activity contains an active verb.
  - Where appropriate, describe what the product or outcome of each activity should be.
  - Specify the tools, materials, approach or method necessary for each activity.

Notes

- If a project contains a large number of activities, consider grouping some activities into subprojects.

- Make sure the project plan contains all the activities needed to achieve the project deliverable (not only those activities done by the project team members).

- Making a good start is always half the battle.

- Almost everything that goes wrong during a project has its origins in the initiation phase.

- Murphy's Law says: There is never enough time to carry out the initiation phase properly the first time around, but always enough to repeat it several times.

Checklist 7.3

Prepare Project Management Plans and Organise Their Progress Control

Every project requires careful management. As the manager responsible for the project, you may need to carry out considerable preparation to make your project manageable. Your success depends on unambiguous management plans. Without these plans, you will find it impossible to identify whether the project is on course. There are only five (no more, no less) perspectives to manage: time, money, quality, release and organisation.

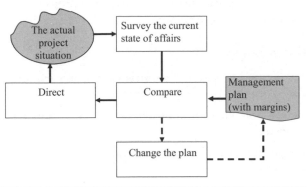

- No progress control possible without margins
- The smaller the margin, the more progress control is needed
- Without management plans (with margins) no statements can be made such as:
  - o taking too long
  - o too expensive
  - o inadequate
  - o in need of change
  - o likely to be unpopular

Figure 7.2   You need to control progress

You can't do anything about deviations from the plan once they have happened.

Managing a project contains two main activities that are mutually dependent: planning and progress control.

- Planning enables you to match the required deliverable against the available means and the work to be done.

- Progress control involves a regular, structured review to determine how far the work in hand threatens to deviate from your original management plans. Whether or not you decide to intervene becomes another important management activity.

It is vitally important to stay within your margin, contingency or float for each of the five management perspectives. Changing your management requirements too often or too easily undermines the credibility of the project manager just as effectively as stubbornly persisting with clearly unrealistic requirements.

Building in margins or contingencies in the management plans is essential to planning projects. Without margins, no management plan is realistic. Using your margins carefully, you can compensate for any minor changes without risking or delaying the project deliverable. A margin is a contingency (positive or negative) that you put in place in response to any potential obstacles or risks you have identified.

Progress control of each management perpective means recording the current state of affairs, comparing this with your management plan and making adjustments to either your plan or the project itself. The aim of your progress control is to allow you to come up with feasible alternatives when faced with the threat of deviations to the management plans. You need creative approaches that will ensure that you still can achieve the desired deliverable. In other words, you should make adjustments so that the project can be carried out in accordance with the management plans.

- *How to control progress:*
    - Work out how often you should monitor each management perspective.
    - Determine how you will monitor them (verbal or written, by hand or computer-aided).
    - Identify the data you need (and make sure it is sufficiently accurate, recent and relevant).
    - Agree who contributes to progress control and when they should do so (who is responsible for comparing reality against the plan and who makes adjustments to the plan or project itself – both in cases where you have margins and in cases that fall outside of them).
    - Advise the project owner to halt the project at any stage that it appears pointless to continue in its present form.

Notes

- Progress control requires trust and candour all round.
- Progress control is all about communicating potential deviations from the management plan.
- Adjustments that come too late are of no use at all.
- Review all the five management perspectives to assess the impact of any change before you decide to implement it.

Checklist 7.4

Manage Your Project Time

You need to manage your time management plan to make sure that all project activities are finished on time, and consequently that the project deliverable is ready on time.

Monitoring your schedule means paying attention to ensure that it is kept to. This is impossible if the right people don't apply the requisite resources at the appropriate time.

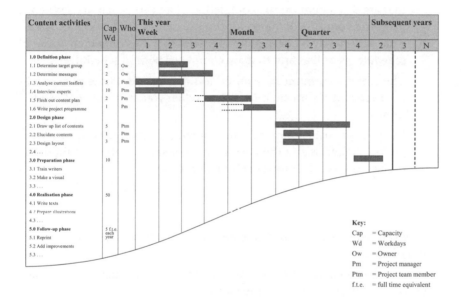

The project deliverable must be ready at the agreed time – 'as soon as possible' just won't do.

Content activities	Cap Wd	Who	This year Week				Month			Quarter			Subsequent years		
			1	2	3	4	2	3	4	2	3	4	2	3	N
1.0 Definition phase															
1.1 Determine target group	2	Ow													
1.2 Determine messages	2	Ow													
1.3 Analyse current leaflets	5	Ptm													
1.4 Interview experts	10	Ptm													
1.5 Flesh out content plan	2	Pm													
1.6 Write project programme	1	Pm													
2.0 Design phase															
2.1 Draw up list of contents	5	Ptm													
2.2 Elucidate contents	1	Ptm													
2.3 Design layout	3	Ptm													
2.4 . . .															
3.0 Preparation phase	10														
3.1 Train writers															
3.2 Make a visual															
3.3 . . .															
4.0 Realisation phase	50														
4.1 Write texts															
4.2 Prepare illustrations															
4.3 . . .															
5.0 Follow-up phase	5 f.t.e. each year														
5.1 Reprint															
5.2 Add improvements															
5.3 . . .															

Key:
Cap = Capacity
Wd = Workdays
Ow = Owner
Pm = Project manager
Ptm = Project team member
f.t.e. = full time equivalent

Figure 7.3   Example of a (GANNT) chart of a project management time plan

- *How to prepare a project management time plan:*

  - Work out the desired completion date for the completed project and any possible interim deliverables (with margins) and identify the start date.

  - Work back from the required project completion date to identify the dates by when each element (or milestone) needs to be completed. Are these dates realistic? If they are not you have three options: (1) negotiate a later project completion date, (2) start the project earlier or (3) negotiate additional resources or people to get the job done faster.

  - Check that your time plan includes margins to cover foreseeable obstacles or hold-ups.

- Make sure you can deploy the right people, in the right numbers, at the right time for each phase of the project. You'll need to consult with the people involved. Don't just assume their compliance.
- Check the availability of equipment, locations or materials (in the same way as the people). You'll need a margin to cover each of these in your time plan.
- Identify the time needed for each of the activities in the project. Make sure that those responsible for the activities understand and commit to the timetable.
- Draw up a project management time plan indicating the start and finish time for each activity against the calendar. Indicate those activities that may be started or worked on concurrently and those that are dependent on the completion of an earlier activity. (When planning your time margins for these activities, have you anticipated what action may be needed for activities that are completed ahead of schedule, as well as any that are completed behind schedule?)
- Check and communicate your project management time plan to all involved and ask for their feedback. When you are ready, publish it formally.
- Use your published project management time plan to control your project's progress and then accelerate or delay activities within the project to meet the project completion date.

Notes

- If a given resource is not available on time, the project deliverable may also be late.
- There is always enough time for rework but seldom enough time to make a good project management time plan.
- Without margins in the project management time plan, it is impossible to ensure that the project will be ready on time.

Checklist 7.5

Manage Your Project Money

Money or financial management involves completing the project activities cost effectively in order to achieve an economical or profitable project.

Progress control of the financial management perspective of a project is not only about the cost-effectiveness and appropriateness of the budget you have already spent but, just as importantly, with the cost-effectiveness and appropriateness of the money still to be spent. After all, you can do little about spent money and sunk costs.

- **How to prepare a project management money plan:**

    - Make a list of the desired/required financial returns (with margins or contingencies).

    - Draw up a cost/benefit analysis, make sure you take into account the views of internal and external stakeholders. Involve those people who will later bear the financial responsibility and, as far as is possible, make sure your analysis runs right up to the end of the life of the project deliverable.

    - Draw up cost frameworks, estimates and a cost budget.

    - Allocate budgets (with contingencies) for subprojects to those responsible for them. These should include:

        - detailed budgets (with narrow contingencies) for the imminent phase of the project;

        - less-detailed budgets (with broader contingencies) for the subsequent phases;

        - an assessed/drawn up financial management plan, formally approved;

        - monitored spending plans, adjusted or re-planned.

Make the project as cost effective or profitable as possible but, more importantly, make it meet its financial target.

Notes

- Money that you have already spent should not play a role in the decision whether or not to go ahead, only the interest to be paid on this capital invested counts.

- Nothing can be done about budgets that have already been exceeded.

- An accurate record of what the project has already cost is not much help to a project manager if the data is already three months old.

Checklist 7.6

Manage Your Project Quality

Quality management involves ensuring that all project activities are carried out appropriately, so that you meet the quality requirements of the project deliverable.

Trials, tests, and assessments as well as quality controls (of interim and final project deliverable) are all facets of quality management. Each phase of a project has its own specific quality control activities.

- *How to prepare a quality management plan:*
  - Determine the quality requirements (with margins) for the project deliverable and ensure that these requirements are recorded.
  - Make sure that the quality requirements are quantified and measurable requirements and are shared with and understood by contributing parties and any subproject teams.
  - Indicate when, how and who must report whether the quality requirements are being met.
  - Assess and present the quality plan and approve it formally.
  - Monitor, adjust or re-plan:
    - During the design phase, test (detailed) designs and prototypes against the project programme baseline document, supervise design reviews and design plans for tools and test procedures.
    - During the preparation phase, make sure that the plans are correctly translated into instructions with the appropriate tools and procedures for testing or manufacturing pilot products.
    - During the realisation phase, carry out tests. Preferable are incoming goods and process tests and as few end-product tests and adjustments as possible.
    - During the follow-up phase, assess complaints and qualify improvements.

Quality means fitness for purpose. It doesn't mean as good as it possibly can be.

Notes

- Checking, testing, controlling, inspecting and assessing are activities that fall within project quality management.
- Self-management is always the best option; enable people to assess and adjust their own work.
- Quality management involves measurable and quantifiable definitions and outcomes and is not the 'with the best practical means' or 'to the best of your ability'. Quality is not what is expected by the customer but what the customer has agreed upon.

Checklist 7.7

Manage Your Project Release

Project release management allows you to carry out all of the project activities in a consistent manner so that you can reach a clear deliverable – one that can be repeated.

There is no controllable truth in a verbal agreement.

Everyone concerned needs to be familiar with and understand the content of the released decision documents.

Formal releasing of documents refers only to those documents that contain the most recent specifications of the project deliverable and the non-managerial project activities. Release management should give you a clear view of the status of any requests for change orders to your project decision documents.

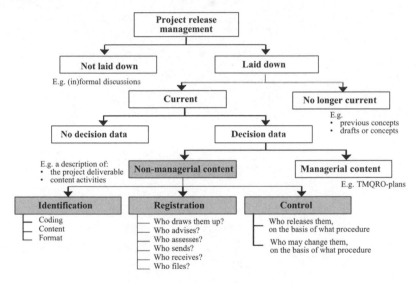

Figure 7.4   Not all project documents need to be managed

- *How to manage the release of project documents:*

  - Design an information management system that describes the decision documents and their content, and that defines how they will be coded for identification, distribution and filing. You need this system in place at the start of the project.

  - Decide who needs to draw up each decision document, who should approve it, file it and have permission to make changes to it.

  - Lay down the procedures for *release* (approval) of and amendments to the decision documents.

  - Draw up the release management plan and approve it formally.

- Control progress, adjust or re-plan.
- Register all requests for changes that have been submitted and make sure a consensus decision to accept or reject the request is made; this decision should be recorded in the relevant decision document.

Notes

- If everyone receives all of the project documents, they will find it impossible to see the wood for the trees. Send only relevant documents to relevant people.
- Once a decision has been made and recorded, this decision is set in stone.
- Project release management has little to do with communication.

Checklist 7.8

Manage Your Project Organisation

Project organisation management ensures that those who are responsible for and authorised to carry out all non-managerial project activities can and will do so and guarantees that the project deliverable will be formally accepted by the project owner.

Controlling progress involves supervising the agreements that cover the division of tasks and the level of authority of all involved in the project. The project manager must monitor communication within the project team and between the project team and external stakeholders.

The project manager is responsible for everyone's level of motivation during the project.

Not: a project owner well satisfied with the project deliverable is what counts, but: a project deliverable as agreed.

- • *How to prepare a project organisation management plan:*

  - • Indicate for whom the project deliverable is intended; who is the project owner? Who is the project manager? Who will carry out the project: the project team members?

  - • Set up a temporary organisation and prepare a family tree to show: who decides what, who is who's manager, who is responsible for carrying out the project activities, how conflicts are to be dealt with, and how additional people will become involved during the course of the project.

  - • Manage the relationships with the external stakeholders of the project (suppliers, financiers) and, if necessary, draw up a communication plan. This plan should include the communication lines between the project owner, stakeholders and users. In addition, indicate the activities in relation to boundary control or interface management, how the external influences (policy, strategy) and external developments (market, technical) are scanned and dealt with.

  - • Put together your project team. Agree how you will work together, how the team will function, the division of roles and internal communication methods.

  - • Prepare the project organisation that will execute the realisation phase.

  - • Draw up and check the organisation management plan and approve it formally.

  - • Control progress, adjust or re-plan (for example, you may need to consider a change to the composition of the team, meeting procedures and the way in which conflicts are dealt with).

Notes

- In order to ensure that the project deliverable is put to best use, the end-users may well require training.
- Cooperation between strangers does not happen without effort.
- Bureaucracy and resistance are strong signals that all is not well with the functioning of the team.

Checklist 7.9

Create the Project Brief

Every project starts with a decision document. In practice, many projects start and end with just this one piece of paper. In professional project management each phase of a project is closed with a baseline or decision document. A decision document is a released starting point that can't be changed without authorisation. The decisions taken at the end and start of each project phase generally involve conscious choices between alternatives. These may include alternative ways of adding details to the project deliverable, to the subsequent project path or the management plans.

The chosen alternative should be a contract between two equal partners – the project owner and the project manager. This contract may only be changed in controlled circumstances.

To illustrate a typical project decision document, here is a checklist for the first decision document, the project brief (also called the project assignment or business case).

- **Format for your project brief**

  1. The project content

     (a) The context of the project: policy, background facts, its relation with other projects, and so on.

     (b) The need and/or goals: the 'why' of the project.

     (c) The deliverable: the 'what is completed when it is completed' of the project.

     (d) The boundaries: the project's demarcation, what it does not include.

     (e) An inventory of risks that define the feasibility of the project.

  2. The phase activities

     (f) A detailed plan of all non-managerial activities for the next phase (the definition phase) of the project.

     (g) A more general plan for all subsequent phases.

  3. The project management plans

     (h) The project time management plan

        – Requirements: expected start date for the project and planned completion date, with margins or contingencies; planned completion date of the definition phase (with narrower margins).

- The number of people expected to be involved in the project at each stage, what kind of role/function and the resources they will require, in detail for the definition phase and more generally for the following phases (in many cases, this time management plan can be designed as a bar chart).

- Description of the method to be used to control progress, indicating who is responsible for controlling the progress of the lead-time; in what way and how frequently the situation will be assessed; how it will be compared to the schedule; who can make adjustments whether within or outside the margins.

(i)   The project money management plan

- Financial requirements: cost estimates (with contingencies); profit-and-loss forecasts or financial targets for the whole project (for example deliverable requirements); detailed budget for the definition phase (with a narrow contingency); less detailed budgets for the following phases (with wider contingency).

- A description of the method to be used to manage the budget indicating who is responsible for financial control, how it is controlled and how frequently the situation will be assessed; how it will be compared to the budget; who can make adjustments (whether within or outside the contingencies).

(j)   Project quality management plan

- Quality requirements: quantified non-managerial requirements (with contingencies) for the project deliverable, including any preconditions. The non-managerial requirements and related quality requirements are not determined until the definition phase. In the initiation phase, they are unlikely to be known. This means you need to describe (in the project brief) who is responsible for and how they will quantify the quality requirements and set up the project quality management plan.

- For every quality requirement: the defined procedure to be used.

- For quality management activities: the description of the progress control method and when the situation will be assessed; how it will be compared to the quality plan; who can make adjustments (whether within or outside the contingencies).

(k) The project release management plan

  – Release requirements: a description of the procedures for coding, classifying, releasing, changing, distributing and filing decision documents.

  – Release management activities: a description of the procedures to ensure that decision documents are formally released; that change procedures for the project brief are carried out; that information in the decision documents is communicated to all involved; that the filing system for the decision documents is determined and organised; that the procedures for publication and change orders are set up.

(l) The project organisation management plan

  – Organisation requirements: a description of the project organisation (tasks, authority and responsibilities of the project owner, project manager and project team members); a description of the relationship between the project organisation and permanent organisation(s) (committees, steering groups, working parties and so on); a description of the procedures for conflict management, delegating and consultations.

  – Organisation management activities: a description of the procedures to ensure that agreements are honoured; that starting-up and adjusting the project organisation can take place; that the next phase can be organised and manned as well as the subsequent phases.

Notes

• A decision document needs to contain the description of the desired project deliverable, all the phase activities and the project management plans.

• The plans need to indicate when decisions are required during the project.

• Make sure the decision-making process does not take such a long time that the schedule has to be amended.

• Check that your project is not simply a vehicle to postpone or avoid a difficult decision.

Executing Your Project – Checklists

When the owner has approved your project brief, then you need to make sure the work that describes it is completed in accordance with your management plans. In project management terms you have completed the initiation phase and are moving to the definition phase.

Your project has been successfully executed when the project deliverable has been accepted by the project owner, made operational and any maintenance and user instructions are in place. Before that, you need to complete the design, preparation and realisation phases.

Each of these phases is started and ended with a decision document. The structure of all decision documents is basically the same, although the content of each subsequent decision document is only detailed and amended as you reach the phase that it describes. The parts of the document that describe the phase activities and management plans share a consistent presentation style for all of the phases (see Figure 8.1).

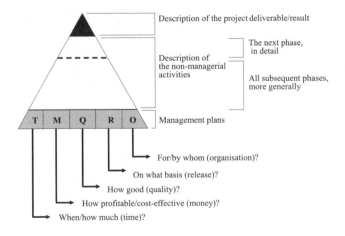

Figure 8.1 Every decision document has the same structure

If a project is made up of six phases, there will be five decision documents. The initiation phase has no start document and the follow-up phase no end document.

A complete decision document is normally made up as follows:

- *Description of the project deliverable* The detail of the description depends on the phase that it is covering. The most detailed description is always to be found in the final decision document: the project follow-up programme.

- *Activities* An overview of all the activities of each phase; in detail for the next phase and more generally for subsequent phases.

- *Project planning and control* A management plan for each of the five management perspectives time, money, quality, release and organisation.

Checklist 8.1

Use Decision Documents

Projects require a decision document at the start and end of each project phase.

Decision making means choosing between alternatives.

Each decision document can be regarded as the formal outcome of all the previous phases and as the plan for the phases to come.

- *How to design a complete decision document:*

  - Make sure that a decision document is complete, specifying the project deliverable, the project plan of the content or phase activities and the management plans for time, money, quality, release and organisation (see Figure 8.1).

  - Make sure that the decision document is designed to encourage acceptance and commitment.

  - Make sure that the decision laid down in the document is reasonable and can be carried out. You could identify the failure or analyse the risks associated with the decision and incorporate these findings into the margins of the management requirements.

  - Organise your decisions in order of importance (most important first!).

  - Make sure that each decision is incorporated into a decision document (a contract or agreement).

Notes

- The signature at the bottom of a decision document is not as important as people's understanding of what is going to happen and their willingness and ability to help carry it out.

- A decision document must be unambiguous. If it isn't you will need to initiate a change order.

- A decision document is never complete; this makes it necessary to have a change procedure.

Checklist 8.2

Carry Out the Definition Phase

The definition phase is designed to create a concrete package of requirements for the intended project deliverable. The specification of the 'what' of the project.

For those who don't know the what, every how is a solution.

These requirements can be grouped into four categories: external interfaces, performance and operational requirements and design constraints.

- *How to prepare a proper project definition:*
  - Gather together the basic information (background, research reports, market studies and so on).
  - Determine the project requirements:
    - external interfaces;
    - performance requirements;
    - operational requirements;
    - design constraints.
  - Check the feasibility of the requirements and eliminate any that are not feasible.
  - Eliminate conflicting requirements.
  - Draw up the second baseline document, called the project programme. In other words, describe the overview of the (phase) activities for each phase in the correct order:
    - a detailed description of the design phase, where necessary describing how these activities will be tackled;
    - a more general description for the remaining phases.
  - Set up the project work breakdown and define the subprojects and the interfaces between them.
  - Set up the content part of the project programme.

Notes

- Avoid vague requirements.
- It is better to have a heated discussion about conflicting requirements now rather than put this off until a later phase.
- A forgotten external interface will always have dramatic consequences for the project.

Checklist 8.3

Prioritise Your Project Requirements

There is a hierarchical order in the project requirements: not every requirement is equally important. The requirements also have a different origin and, what is more, they have different purposes.

A distinction is often made between different types of requirements:

The project requirements determine the 'what' of the project deliverable.

- External interface requirements which cannot be influenced from within the project and which the project deliverable must meet unconditionally. These requirements stem from the (future) environment, such as laws, natural conditions, prevailing policy, contiguous projects, a programme, the existing or planned infrastructure.

- Functional requirements which define the performance of the project. Functional requirements, also known as 'features' or 'characteristics', are related to the project's rationale; the reason why it was started in the first place, the reason why the project owner is supporting it.

- Operational requirements and wishes relating to the application and the use of the project deliverable. These requirements usually come from the users (for example machine operators, car drivers and book readers).

- Design constraint requirements and wishes directed towards accomplishing the result. The goal is to make everyone aware of existing tools and preferred solutions. These are often provided by the 'makers'.

When identifying and arranging project requirements during the definition phase of a project, it is important to be thorough, concrete and clear. Focus on the purpose, significance and origin of the requirements.

- ***How to identify and prioritise the project requirements:***

  - Determine the external influences: requirements that the project deliverable must meet unconditionally, including the relationship with the relevant environment.

  - Specify the performance requirements: what must the project deliverable achieve, what it must do or cause to be done; seek the requirements of the project owner, these requirements can often be deduced from the project goals.

  - Specify the operational requirements by indicating what the users/ clients can, will or must do with the project deliverable; users also include those who must support and maintain the project deliverable.

  - Specify the design constraints by finding out what those who are making the project deliverable will use.

Type of requirement \ Type of project	Job rating system	Computer system
External interface	Existing social policy Existing assessment system	Existing computer hardware
Functional requirement	Across-the-board salary increase of no more than 2% Complaints under 10%	Required data available by the 6th working day of the new period at the latest
Operational requirement	Each supervisor should be able to explain the system	Output covering no more than six A4 sheets
Design constraint	Using existing assessment committee	Name and logo of the users on each output form

Figure 8.2   Examples of project requirements

Notes

- A vague requirement is no requirement.
- Don't accept any requirements that are not feasible.
- Requirements must not conflict.
- The external interfaces have the highest priority followed in descending order by performance requirements, operational requirements and design constraints.

Checklist 8.4

Define Subprojects

Sometimes a project can be of such a size that it is handy to divide it up into a number of subproject or constituent projects. At other times, constituent projects must be formulated in order to make it possible for each organisation involved to participate. There are various classification principles for subdividing projects into their constituent parts.

Using subprojects often makes it easier to retain an overview of the whole project as well as giving an insight into it. Realising subprojects demands that all their relevant interfaces (or the relationships between them) are unambiguously specified as well as requiring very close monitoring of the interfaces against unauthorised and inadvertent changes. Subprojects offer a useful opportunity to check the completeness of the project – that all the correct parts have been included.

Examples Division criteria	A construction project	A report
Object-oriented	• The building • The garden • The inventory	• Cover • Page dividers • Pages
Discipline-oriented	• Architecture • Installation technique • Landscaping	• Legal • Socio-economic • Financial
Sequence-oriented	• Building • Completion • Furnishing	• Writing • Printing • Distribution
Performance-oriented	• Leisure activities • Hobbies • Household activities	• Reading activities • Decision-making activities • Filing activities
Geography-oriented	• Ground floor • First floor • Attic	• Foreword and introduction • Chapter 1-n • Appendices

Figure 8.3   Examples of subprojects within a main project

- *How to create subprojects:*
  - Subprojects are groups of activities within a project that logically belong together, on the basis that:
    - finetuning with other subprojects is relatively simple;
    - finetuning within a subproject is usually based on experience and know-how.
  - You may create subprojects along any of the following lines for example:
    - object-oriented;

- discipline-oriented;
- sequence-oriented;
- performance-oriented;
- geography-oriented.
- Specify each subproject:
  - translate and assign the project requirements for the subproject;
  - specify all the relationships between the subprojects, requirements and activities.

Notes

- The greater the number of subprojects, the more relationships between them there will be to manage.
- The greater the number of subprojects, the greater the number of activities that can be carried out simultaneously.
- Logically organised subprojects may not always fit seamlessly into the existing structure of organisations or departments participating in the project.

Checklist 8.5

Realise Your Management Plans

Management is only possible if agreements about each of the five management perspectives have been made and recorded. To achieve your project you need to record the completion date, available time and money, who does what, how good the project deliverable must be and so on. Without these agreements and a clear record of them, it is impossible to refer back to your plans or objectives once the project is under way. The only thing that is certain in the course of a project is that the project will change along the way. These changes will happen at the end of each phase, and then as often as is necessary or useful. The idea that we've got a project time management plan and it is written in stone is dangerous. The various management plans must be regularly tested and adjusted, at an agreed frequency. At the very least you need to double check the viability of your plans at the transition stage between project phases to see whether some fine tuning is required.

Management should follow the management cycle for every management plan: plan, do, check and act. For actualising a management plan the following has to be done.

- **How to actualise the management plans:**

    - (Re)define the management requirement and how is it to be achieved.

    - (Re)define the management plans for the phase activities within the current phase of the project.

    - Re-assess the principles and procedures for progress control.

    - Re-assess how (and by whom) information of the current state of play will be communicated through progress reports (you need to compare where you are now with where you ought to be).

    - (Re)define authorisation and adjust responsibilities, both within and outside the various margins or contingencies.

Notes

- Ensure that management plans are laid down unambiguously.
- Ensure that in each of the plans for the five management perspectives there is:
    - a stated management requirement with contingencies/margins;
    - a process for planning as well as a plan;

- a procedure for progress control.
- Progress reports need to be trustworthy, independent and forward-looking.

Checklist 8.6

Create the Project Programme Decision Document

The same factors that apply to the project brief also apply to the project programme.

- ***How to create your project programme decision document***

  - Record the requirements of your project deliverable items in terms of:

    - external interfaces (external requirements);

    - performance requirements (functions and characteristics);

    - operational requirements (usage, support and maintenance);

    - design constraints (preferred solutions from the team members).

  - Record any subprojects.

  - Note which requirements are linked with which subprojects.

  - Note the relationship between the various subprojects.

  - Draw up the project plan including:

    - a detailed plan for the design phase of all non-managerial activities;

    - a more general plan for the other phases.

  - Record the outcome of the various management activities carried out during the definition phase. These should be grouped per management perspective (time, money, quality, release and organisation) and the record should include:

    - the management requirement, with margins or contingencies;

    - the relevant management plans;

    - the agreed procedures for progress control.

If you have no idea of what you need to achieve, there is no point in carrying on.

Notes

- A project programme document is a living document that you need to update on a regular basis to record decisions and new agreements as you reach them.

- A project programme document that needs constant fundamental change is likely to prove unworkable.

- The project programme document should include enough information to define 80% to 85% of how the project will run.

Checklist 8.7

Design Your Project

The design phase involves creating a completed and detailed solution or design for the project deliverable.

- *How to design your project:*

  - Detail the project programme.
  - Investigate which elements to create in-house and which elements to buy-in from outside.
  - Design each subproject or look for already existing designs or solutions.
  - Look for existing project tools (or design new ones).
  - Gear subproject solutions to match the project requirements.
  - Adjust the subproject designs when they have been checked, tested or tried out.
  - Draw up the definitive, detailed project design for:
    - each of the subprojects;
    - each of the project tools.
  - Draw up the project plan; describe and adjust the overview of the phase activities in the correct sequence for each phase of the project including:
    - a detailed description of the preparation phase, where necessary describing how each of the activities will be tackled;
    - a more general description for the remaining phases.
  - Describe the design of the project and the work for the next phases.

It's not about how you tackle the project, but what the project deliverable will look like.

Notes

- What you are trying to do should determine how you do it and not vice versa.
- A good design is one that can be made, used, kept, maintained and thrown out at the end of the project life cycle.
- Avoid the temptation for endless tinkering with the design; it needs to be completed within an agreed timescale.

Checklist 8.8

Create Your Project Design Decision Document

You need to understand clearly what the project deliverable looks like, before you go any further.

The project design document originates in much the same way as the two previously mentioned decision documents: the project brief and the project programme.

- *How to create your project design document:*
    - Draw up detailed design plans; such as the technical drawings, a detailed lists of contents or a layout:
        - for the whole project;
        - for each subproject.
    - Draw up parts lists for every design.
    - Describe the realisation methods (qualitative).
    - Describe the realisation tools (quantitative).
    - Draw up the project plan including:
        - a detailed plan of all non-managerial activities for the preparation phase;
        - a more general plan for subsequent phases.
    - Record the outcome of the various management activities carried out during the design phase for each of the five management perspectives (in other words, actualise the management plans):
        - the management requirements, including margins or contingencies;
        - the relevant management plans;
        - the relevant procedures for progress control.

Notes

- The project design demands precision.
- All materials, tools and aids that play a role in the making, implementing, using, monitoring and replacing of the project deliverable need to be described in this decision document.
- The project design document should define 95% of the way in which the project will run.

Checklist 8.9

Do the Project Preparation Phase

The preparation phase of your project is geared to gaining an exact description of the project deliverable which will then help you implement it smoothly.

- ***How to do the preparation phase of your project:***
    - Work out the detailed design in implementation plans, production plans and procedures, and so on.
    - Draw up instructions for how the plan should be realised.
    - Buy in or design all the necessary tools.
    - Contact and instruct third parties, contractors or suppliers.
    - Draw up the project plan; in this case, describe and adjust the overview of the non-managerial activities in the correct sequence for each phase of the project including:
        - a detailed description of the realisation phase; where necessary describing how these activities will be tackled;
        - a more general description for the remaining follow-up phase.
    - Describe the project realisation programme and the work of the next phases.

Notes

- Be well prepared.
- Check and recheck your assumptions.
- Anticipate the possible and allow for the impossible.

To get it right first time requires foresight.

Checklist 8.10

Create the Realisation Programme Decision Document

This decision document originates in much the same way as the three previously mentioned decision documents: the project brief, the project programme and the project design document.

- ***How to create the realisation programme decision document for your project:***

Make sure you have anticipated all of the pitfalls.

  - Draw up the deliverable drawings and procedures (product and production specifications and so on).
  - Make a list of the specified deliverable components, parts or elements.
  - Make a note of the inventory lists of tools and other appliances.
  - Describe the realisation methods or production processes (qualitative).
  - Describe the realisation tools (quantitative).
  - Draw up the purchasing specifications/contracts with third parties.
  - Draw up the project plan including a detailed plan of the activities:
    - for the realisation phase;
    - a more general plan for the last phase: the follow-up phase.
  - Record the outcome of the various management activities carried out for each of the management perspectives during the preparation phase:
    - the management requirements, with contingencies;
    - the relevant management plans;
    - the relevant agreements and procedures for monitoring progress.

Notes

- If you don't know what the project deliverable looks like, don't even start this stage.
- A realisation programme document is always work-in-progress.
- The project realisation programme decision document should define 99.5% of the way in which the project will run.

Checklist 8.11

Realise Your Project Deliverable

The realisation phase is aimed at achieving a perfect project deliverable in one go.

- *How to realise your project:*

  - Contract all third party suppliers and contractors.
  - Follow the realisation programme.
  - Draw up the technical documents for the follow-up phase detailing the use/operation and maintenance of the project deliverable.
  - Draw up any procedures for transport and installation or reinstallation of the project deliverable.
  - Train the users, the support and maintenance staff.
  - Draw up a project plan to this phase; detail and adjust the overview of the phase activities in the follow-up phase up to the end of the follow-up phase (when the project result or deliverable does not exist any more) in the correct order; where necessary describe how these activities will be tackled.
  - Set up the content part for the follow-up programme.

Notes

- The project deliverable must be completely finalised at the end of this phase.
- The realisation phase represents the implementation of your project deliverable.
- The use, support, maintenance and demolition of the project deliverable must now be completely in place.

Stay focussed on what you promised to realise and not on what you want to realise.

Checklist 8.12

Create the Project Follow-up Programme Decision Document

It is only done when everything is completed as agreed.

The final decision document should cover the life of the project deliverable. It is the beginning of the ongoing follow-up phase.

*   *How to prepare the follow-up programme decision document:*

    *   Draw up the 'as carried out' schemes (revision documents, 'as built' drawings and so on).

    *   Make the 'as carried out' parts lists.

    *   Draw up a detailed project plan for the follow-up phase:

        *   the user manual;

        *   the support and maintenance instructions;

        *   the instructions for dismantling and so on.

    *   Record the outcome of the management activities carried out for each of the five management perspectives during the realisation phase:

        *   the management requirements, with contingency;

        *   the relevant management plans;

        *   the relevant agreements for monitoring progress.

Notes

*   Do not proceed unless the complete project deliverable, including a completed and endorsed follow-up programme is available.

*   Any adjustments to help those using and supporting the deliverable must be recorded and documented; otherwise, in a short while, no one will have any idea what has been completed.

*   Now is the time to reflect on what you can learn from the project.

Checklist 8.13

Do the Follow-Up Phase

The follow-up phase is all about using and supporting the project deliverable.

The whole project finds its ultimate justification in the follow-up phase. This phase should run as planned, pursuing the project goals or diminishing the problems stated at the start of your project.

- ***How to follow-up your project:***
    - Use the project deliverable.
    - Support the project deliverable.
    - Maintain the project deliverable and the project tools.
    - Improve and modify the project deliverable and the tools.
    - Optimise the use, care and maintenance of the project deliverable.
    - Demolish, destroy or replace the project deliverable.

Notes

- The follow-up phase is the most important phase of all.
- The project in the broader sense starts with the beginning of the initiation phase and ends with the ending of the follow-up phase.
- In many projects it will not be clear exactly how and when the follow-up phase is complete.

The project deliverable must last for the rest of its life cycle.

Checklist 8.14

Take the Temperature of Your Project

As a project manager you will want to know, for your own peace of mind as well as for your project owner and other stakeholders, how the project is progressing. In many cases, regular progress control will suffice. But in exceptional circumstances, such as the appearance of new, unexpected internal or external opportunities or threats, a special health check may be needed.

It is also not unusual for an internal or external stakeholder to ask for an explicit update on the project's progress – what's been done and what remains to be done.

Project health checks are usually aimed at pinpointing as many potential bottlenecks or stumbling blocks as possible in a relatively short time.

This form of assessment is structured and finely targeted and requires the cooperation of all those involved. Checking the health of your project can be done at any time.

A project health check may not necessarily mean that everything comes to light.

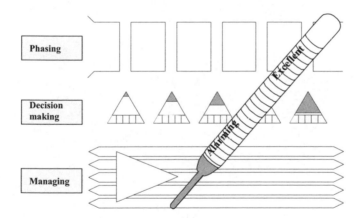

Figure 8.4   Assessing a project is like measuring the temperature of your body

- *How to health check your project:*
  - Become familiar with the project in question; gaining access to the relevant people and documents.
  - Gather information from both people and documents; check the history of the project to date and gather information about future expectations.

- Check the description of the desired project deliverable for ambiguity with those concerned, and the completeness of the current project phase.
- Check the phases in the project plan that have yet to be carried out for completeness and feasibility.
- Check the management plans for their attention to detail, their usefulness and whether there are sufficient margins or contingencies in place.
- Draw up your prognosis of the project; that is, the likelihood that it will deliver on time, within budget, with the required quality, according to the released and up-to-date specifications and accepted by the project owner.

Notes

- It is impossible to carry out a good health check without the cooperation of everyone involved.
- Your project health check should form the basis of any remedial action.
- The checking process itself can improve the health of a project.

Checklist 8.15

Have Your Project Audited

A project audit is a systematic and independent project investigation carried out to determine if a project is being professionally and sensibly approached and managed.

An audit also provides an insight into the likelihood of success of the rest of the project. The results of an audit should provide a set of specific and detailed proposals for action.

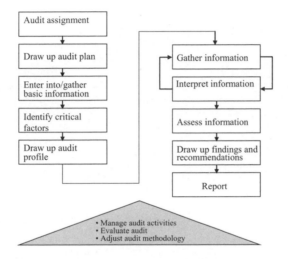

Figure 8.5   Project auditing is a well-structured process

What does an independent third party think of your project?

- ***How to establish a project audit:***

  - Determine the shape of the audit – the rationale, depth, focus and outcome requirements.

  - Make the auditor or the audit team draw up a rough audit plan covering the following aspects – goal/scope, planned stages/approach and those involved/audit organisation, audit manager and audit owner.

  - Ask the auditor or the audit team to gather together basic information about the project; the latest valid project specifications, activities and management plans.

  - Ask the auditor or the audit team to identify the project's critical success and failure factors.

  - Ask the auditor or the audit team to draw up the audit plan in detail and ensure that conditions and tools are in place to carry it out.

- Ask the auditor or the audit team to collect, interpret and appraise the necessary project information for the plan, from interviews or documents.

- Ask the auditor or the audit team to compile the audit report (containing their findings and recommendations) and present it.

Notes

- People often feel that a project evaluation also evaluates them.

- The reality of a project is not always the same as someone's perception of it.

- You need the cooperation of those evaluated during a project audit.

Checklist 8.16

Have Your Project Reviewed

A project review is an internal, forward-looking meeting attended by the main stakeholders.

A project review has two aims: firstly, to bring everyone up-to-date on the project's latest developments and, secondly, to involve everyone in the decision-making process about the project's future.

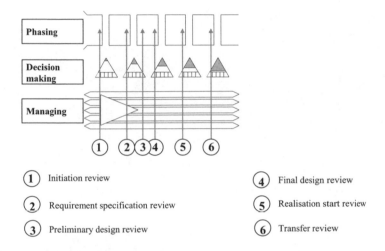

(1) Initiation review
(2) Requirement specification review
(3) Preliminary design review
(4) Final design review
(5) Realisation start review
(6) Transfer review

Figure 8.6   You can review each phase of a project

- *How to review your project:*

  - Draw up the agenda for the review meeting (items, sequence, time and participants).

  - Come to the meeting well prepared; make it clear what is expected of everyone and encourage an open and supportive process.

  - Ensure that issues are thoroughly aired, that potential bottlenecks are discussed in depth and that everyone is involved in finding solutions.

  - During the course of the review ensure that the relationships or interfaces between subprojects and between the project deliverable and the relevant environment of the project are respected.

  - Ensure that the minutes of the review are clear and precise, and that decisions and agreements are phrased unambiguously.

  - Ensure that the agreements are carried out correctly according to established progress monitoring procedures.

Reviewing each phase prevents the project's failure.

Notes

- A project review is designed to reiterate the main points of the project.
- A third party who takes on the role of devil's advocate can be very useful in a project review.
- Some sponsors demand at least one review for each phase of the project.

Checklist 8.17

Evaluate Your Project

Post-project evaluation is only worthwhile if the lessons learned are incorporated into new projects.

A degree of scepticism is not out of place in view of the fact that every project is unique in terms of such things as people involved, deliverables, commitment, circumstances and environment. However, post-project evaluation is well worthwhile for people who work together intensively on similar projects.

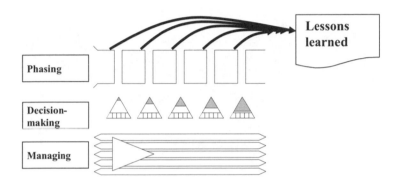

It is easy to be wise after the event.

Figure 8.7   You can always learn lessons from your project

- ***How to evaluate your project:***

  - Make sure that holding a post-evaluation is worthwhile or necessary, that it is not a witch-hunt, that it is not being held too late in the day, or simply because it is always done.
  - Identify what is to be investigated, and how.
  - Collate and evaluate relevant information and opinions.
  - Draw up a list of the lessons learned and distribute it to those who should and those who express a wish to learn from them.
  - Organise a lessons-learned session to discuss the evaluation and the individual lessons to be learned from it.

Notes

- People will only learn something if they are motivated to do so.
- Post evaluation can quickly degenerate into a platform for venting anger and mutual recrimination. This teaches people little that will help them in a subsequent project.

- Post-project evaluation must be carried out by and with the people who worked on the project.

9

Managing Your Programme – The Approach

A 'programme' is a unique set of goals that have been agreed in advance and that must be pursued with limited means and a unique and complex set of activities. A programme as such does not exist. Managers taking together a number of specific, unique and temporary, goal-oriented efforts that must be achieved with limited means call them a programme. In doing so, they should accept the consequences of needing to make rules and agreements contrary to their normal practice. But, more importantly, they should agree to work using a programme-oriented management 'method'. This chapter deals with that method: the language, rules of the game and the make-up of a programme. Of course, the methodology side of programme management cannot and must not be seen as being separate from the other key processes of working together in teams and organising all involved.

There are a dozen basic rules for professional programme management:

1. Those involved recognise that 'routine' tasks need to be managed differently from special or 'one-off' assignments: Agreement needs to be reached on the goals, efforts, means and approach of each programme (unlike routine work, where this only has to be done sporadically).
2. There is a division between who is responsible for the formulation of and the pursuit of the goals and those responsible for delivering the outcome (the first is the responsibility of the programme owner while the second rests with the programme manager).
3. Those involved can use the programme to pursue a variety of goals, as long as these are part of the agreed outcome and are consistent with the means required to achieve it.
4. There is only one programme owner – someone who must be capable of taking decisions on essential choices during the programme. This ensures that management and decision making are substantially simplified and speeded up.
5. The programme owner must ensure that the goals are pursued, but more especially that the desired outcome is defined in advance. They also need to make all the necessary means available – personnel, finance, materials and other resources.

6. The task of ensuring that the right things are done is the responsibility of the programme owner. The programme manager then makes sure that these are carried out correctly.
7. The programme owner and programme manager should involve the programme team members as early as possible, because the sooner they are involved, the more committed they will be to the implementation of the programme.
8. Users and maintenance staff should be involved in the programme at an early stage.
9. The programme manager and programme owner need to ensure that their programme fulfils the characteristics of a programme – unique assignment, flexible, important to those involved, clear goals and outcome oriented.
10. The programme is managed by focussing on the four processes of programme management – the stakeholders, organising, team working and method.
11. Before the programme manager can get down to work, they need to ensure there is agreement between the stakeholders about the programme plan. This involves attention to the goals, support for the management plans for the tempo, feasibility, efficiency, flexibility and goal orientation.
12. The sponsor should be ready to take the decision to close or continue the programme at key milestones and particularly at the end of specific stages.

Programme management has often proven to be useful when a large number of closely linked projects and other efforts or activities need to be carried out within or between organisations – for example when an organisation is temporarily engaged in the pursuit of certain strategic goals or when an assignment becomes so complex that it can no longer be overseen. But programme management can also be useful for merging goals that are, in fact, contradictory; for example improved efficiency of a railway must be merged with improved railway safety.

Programme management can also be used for those unique assignments where a large number of relationships between the relevant efforts have to be closely geared to one another. This situation requires a different, more appropriate management method to bring this complex unique assignment to a satisfactory conclusion.

Our programme management method can be applied to both internal programmes and external programmes (carried out for external clients).

The 12 common characteristics of our programme management methodology are:

1. thinking and acting with the programme goals, their impact and outcome in mind;
2. thinking first (from the big picture to the details), then acting;
3. distinguishing between content activities (non-managerial) and managerial ones (managing tempo, feasibility, efficiency, flexibility and goal-orientation);

4. ensuring you have a systematic start-up, implementation and shut down of your programme;
5. making a list of all non-managerial activities and the sequence (stage) in which they need to be tackled;
6. drawing up and seeking approval for a management plan covering the five perspectives of tempo, feasibility, efficiency, flexibility and goal-orientation before you start (taking into account the risks associated with the contingencies you establish for each) and the continuous progress control of these plans;
7. opting to stop or continue in the interim, based in part on the current programme plan;
8. integrating the outcome of the previous stage with the forecast of the efforts that have to be implemented in the next stage or stages and any required adjustments to the five management perspectives in a programme plan;
9. clearly delegating tasks, responsibilities and authority;
10. controlling management of changes to the programme plans;
11. involving interested parties at the right time and on the right issues;
12. taking decisions, based upon the programme plan at the end of each stage, that opt for continuation or termination of the programme.

Only one thing can be predicted with absolute certainty in programme management: circumstances will change. New stakeholders will want to be involved, the powers that be will lose interest or third parties will realise outcomes that make some of your programme efforts no longer relevant or necessary. Changes will take place both in and around the programme. Some programme efforts will be curtailed, others will be slowed down and yet others will be initiated. Goals will be adjusted, redefined and added to and some goals will be dropped.

All these changes can only be managed if the goals being pursued and their associated efforts have been recorded unambiguously. Only then can you be sure exactly how you need to respond to certain information. You will know, for example, if and how to react to changes in the balance of power. Your management plan, if properly documented, will enable you to judge the consequences and push through all the proposed and necessary changes relatively quickly.

The programme management method consists of three main processes: programming, managing and decision making:

- *Programming* involves the specification of the programme's goals, of the non-managerial efforts needed to achieve these and of the means needed. The key activity in programming is carrying out the specified efforts, those efforts that are logical and vital for pursuing the specified programme goals.
- *Managing* entails planning and progress monitoring your management plans. The management plan for each management perspective is based on the goals to be pursued, the efforts needed and the means available.

- *Decision making* is the final part of the process. The results of programming and managing are integrated in a programme plan. The programme plan must be unambiguous and consistent. Preparing a programme plan involves drawing up plans and seeking, forming and making decisions in response to these plans. Programme plans will have to be drawn up at regular, predetermined intervals and at the start and finish of each programme stage.

PROGRAMMING: NOT JUST THINKING, BUT DOING

In the programme method, the ER-goals are further defined or broken down in MACIC or SMART goals. An ER-goal is the desired state, quality or characteristic of an object in a specific environment – an unattainable ideal worth striving for. Some examples of ER-goals are: a bettER consultation within our committee, a nicER building for our accommodation in France, friendliER behaviour from our receptionists to our clients, a bettER transport system in London city, a biggER market share for our cellphones in China. The acronym MACIC means Measurable, Acceptable, Committing, Inspiring and Communicated. The acronym SMART means Specific, Measurable, Acceptable, Realisable and Traceable. This is done to be able to pursue these broken down goals by programming, that is, listing, charting, grouping and carrying out all the requisite non-managerial efforts.

One or more efforts is linked to each measurable goal or subgoal in such a way that it is clear how much any particular effort contributes to a specific goal. In many cases, the goals and the efforts necessary to pursue them can be represented in the form of a diagram, a goals/efforts network (GEN).

The process of linking alternatively goals with efforts and visa versa often gives a more complete and easily defendable and/or substantiated GEN. This process of alternation makes it increasingly clear exactly what the programme is about. The commitment to goals, their priorities and boundaries can also increase dramatically if the GEN is constructed in collaboration with the most prominent members of the programme team and the most important advocates of its goals.

Those charged with carrying out the programme's specified efforts must be involved with the composition of the goals/efforts/means network (GEM). When compiling a GEM (see the example in Figure 9.1) you need to consider which resources are required and which are then available for each programmed effort. Resources can include manpower, but also space, machines and desks as well as consumables. These resources can be specified in terms of quantity or in terms of their exact make-up, as required.

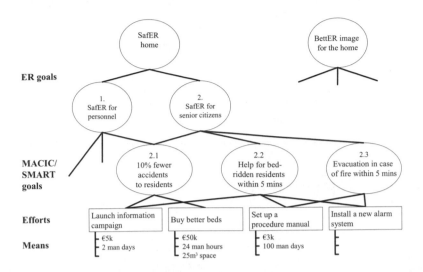

Figure 9.1 Goals/efforts/means network

Once completed, a GEM can often be reproduced on a single sheet of A4, which makes it a perfect instrument for communication between all the parties involved in the programme.

A well-compiled GEM can demonstrate which interfaces are considered to be important between the various efforts; for example, by indicating the degree to which any given effort contributes to the pursuit of any given goal. Once a GEM is set up it can then be adjusted, extended or adapted as necessary (in a controlled manner however). The GEM forms one of the essential blueprints by which decisions can be made. Of course, a GEM is also a handy and useful tool for the programme manager to illustrate the natural and logical sequence of the non-managerial efforts that have to be carried out with the associated specified resources.

For easy reference, it is usually necessary to bring the various efforts together in a programme structure; this is known as clustering (see Figure 9.2). Clustering can be done in many different ways. Sometimes clusters are made up on the basis of the parties involved; sometimes it is easier to categorise the efforts by discipline, source of finance, target group or geographical area.

Obviously, the whole point of programming is to carry out all the non-managerial efforts relevant to the programme.

A programme has a life cycle with three stages: start-up, implementation and shutdown (see Figure 9.3). In programmes, the transition from one stage to the next is a natural but always pragmatic moment when formal decisions about the programme are made.

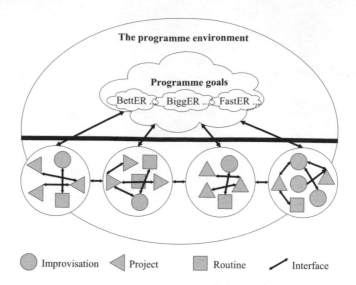

Figure 9.2 Clustering a programme

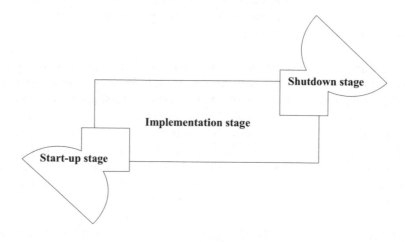

Figure 9.3 Stages in a programme life cycle

The division between the three stages is marked by programme plans, but these plans will be reviewed and updated whenever necessary during each stage.

The following are typical of the questions addressed during the *start-up stage*:

- Which stakeholders (individuals, organisations or parts of organisations) are involved in implementing the programme? Who is not involved?

- Which goals do the stakeholders wish to pursue jointly and which goals are excluded?

- Which non-managerial efforts belong in the programme, and which do not?

- Why have these efforts been integrated into a programme? Why haven't they been tackled routinely, as simple work activities, or been integrated into a major project?

The programme grows during the *implementation stage.* The number of projects and other efforts gradually increase, as do the energy and resources being deployed. The programme reaches maturity during this stage.

The *shutdown stage* offers three possibilities: stopping, dividing or transferring.

Stopping a programme entails carefully winding up the activities that still need to be carried out. If the programme is divided into several new ones, the new programmes must be built up at the same time as the original programme is shut down. In this way, it is possible to create one or more new programmes out of the original, each with their own life cycle. Dividing or transferring a programme means that the programme is effectively shut down. All the programme results and remaining efforts are transferred to the relevant stakeholders to be pursued independently. Alternatively all the programme efforts may be brought together into a new, permanent organisational unit.

MANAGING GOAL-ORIENTED EFFORTS

Managing a programme ensures not only that all the outcomes and interim results from previously documented efforts make the required contribution to the programme, but that all the interfaces within the programme, and between the programme and its relevant environment, are managed and respected.

Management is not about carrying out the non-managerial efforts but about creating the conditions to make carrying them out possible. To this end, management plans need to be drawn up to control the progress of these (content) efforts.

The main programme management tasks include general managerial activities such as inspiring and motivating people and initiating, coordinating and ending routine activities within the programme. This often requires the programme manager to take on the role of (delegated) programme sponsor when working with project managers and department heads.

A programme manager needs perspectives or criteria in a programme that help them to prioritise and compare dissimilar items. In principle, these perspectives can be redefined for each new programme. Programme management usually distinguishes five management perspectives, making integral management of the programme possible: tempo, feasibility, efficiency,

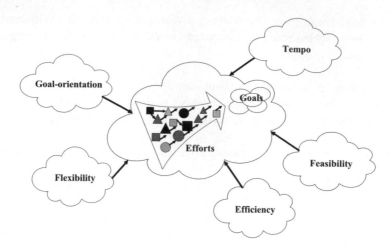

Figure 9.4   Management perspectives of programme management

flexibility and goal-orientation (see Figure 9.4). Using these perspectives, the programme manager is able to compare the various non-managerial efforts and determine how far each is appropriate in view of the overall goals and the context of the programme.

These criteria also offer us the opportunity to evaluate and compare progress for the programme's various efforts, which enables a considered decision on whether or not to adjust the programme to be taken.

The five perspectives are defined as follows:

- *Tempo* From this perspective it is possible to measure and assess the programme's progress, and particularly the pace and timing of a programme effort needed to produce the desired outcome when required. The earlier you can complete a given effort, the more attractive that effort will be from the tempo perspective.

- *Feasibility* Feasibility is a programme management perspective that estimates the degree of risk of any given effort realising or falling short of the contribution that is expected of it. Programme activities which have the greatest potential for moving you towards your goals must be given the highest priority.

- *Efficiency* The efficiency perspective enables programme management to compare the probable financial value of the programme efforts. The fewer resources needed to carry out an effort, or the greater its potential return or effect, the greater its contribution.

- *Flexibility* Flexibility is the programme management perspective designed to assess the versatility of the effort in question. This flexibility is often demonstrated by the speed with which an effort can be curtailed or changed. It also becomes apparent in the way in which capacities and resources can be transferred from one effort to another with the minimum of fuss. Efforts that take up the lion's share of the programme's capacities must be carefully managed.

- *Goal-orientation* This perspective allows you to measure how far programme efforts can contribute to the stated goals. Of course, highly goal-oriented efforts are preferable.

The value allocated to the various perspectives will vary with each programme. In one programme, feasibility may be high on the list, whilst in another flexibility will be considered to be the most valuable. To be able to manage a programme on this basis you need to determine the value of each of the perspectives in relation to the others. This could be achieved by assigning a particular weighting factor to each perspective.

Of course, all the management perspectives of a programme are linked. An effort that is inflexible and that takes a long time (thus scoring badly on the tempo perspective) but that appears to be extremely goal oriented and enjoys wide support could be lower scoring than a flexible and goal-oriented effort that has narrower support.

If the perspectives of a programme are given specific measures of practicality and weighting factors, the programme manager will be able to judge each non-managerial effort on the basis of the perspectives.

Progress control is the second crucial element in programme management. Progress can only be controlled if timely, reliable, complete and, in particular, forward-looking information on progress is received from the various contributors to the programme. All the relevant information from the programme's environment also needs to be timely, reliable, complete and forward-looking.

DECISION MAKING: CHOOSING GOALS AND THE CONSEQUENCES

The start of a programme is normally invisible and, for this reason, can appear simple – but appearances can be deceptive. The start-up stage of a programme, which entails determining the GEM, constructing the programme organisation and searching for and recording management criteria, is anything but easy.

To prevent any programme being carried out blindly, unnecessarily or wrongly, conscious choices need to be made during its life to continue, adjust or stop it. The programme owner needs to be provided with plans that require a decision, at regularly agreed intervals. This frequency will be higher during the start-up stage than in the middle of the implementation stage, and will increase again during the shutdown stage.

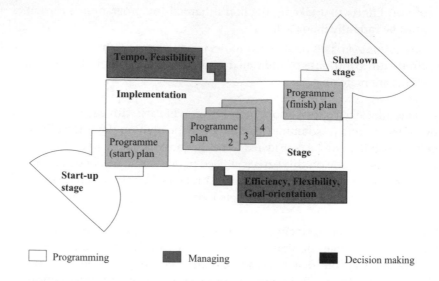

Programming   Managing   Decision making

Figure 9.5   Programme management integrates programming, management and decision making

By taking a decision based on the proposed programme plan, the programme owner either accepts or rejects what has been achieved up to that time and either accepts or rejects the programme manager's plans for the efforts for the coming stages.

This will involve not only plans for the five management perspectives, but should also include plans for staff capacity, financial profit and loss, performance and communication.

Figure 9.5 shows a schematic description of this programme management method, where programming, managing and decision making are integrated processes.

We hope that we made it clear that programme management is not suitable for managers who enjoy freedom from obligation, political opportunism or helpless dependence.

CHAPTER 10

Starting and Executing Your Programme – Checklists

You can use the checklists in this chapter to start, specify, manage and control the progress of your programme. You will have executed your programme successfully when the programme outcomes are accepted by the owner, made operational and all maintenance and user instructions are provided for. By then you will have completed the start-up, implementation and shutdown stages of your programme.

Most programmes involve many people from very different organisations. Frequently these people are all pursuing different, sometimes conflicting, goals. A programme begins by determining these goals. As long as these have not been specified sufficiently clearly, carrying out any non-managerial effort is a risky business. Good goal specification is the basis of a good programme plan. And this process is an important part of the start-up stage of the programme.

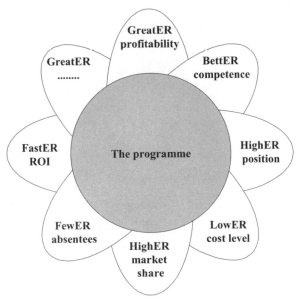

Figure 10.1   A programme serves various (conflicting) goals

You will need to avoid or overcome several pitfalls when starting and executing your programme:

- It may not be clear what does not belong in the programme; the programme boundaries have yet to been determined.
- The target groups, users and 'victims' may not have been identified and are often changing their opinions and positions.
- No analysis may have been made of the relevant players in the environment.
- The programme may have little or no support.
- Only the interesting work has been recognised by those taking part in the programme.

Checklist 10.1

Carry Out the Start-Up Stage

The start-up stage of a programme is all about reaching agreement with all the stakeholders.

Look before you leap.

Consult and reflect on the nature, scale, importance and boundaries of the specified programme before you set these parameters in stone.

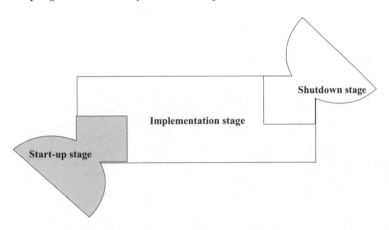

Figure 10.2 The start-up stage of a programme

- *How to carry out the start-up stage of your programme:*

    - Start by formulating the goals and subgoals for the programme.

    - Determine the programme's boundaries – what does not belong in the programme.

    - Formulate all the non-managerial efforts aimed at pursuing the goals.

    - Construct a goals/efforts network (GEN) and subsequently a goals/efforts/means network (GEM).

    - Cluster the efforts and identify the relationships and overlaps (interfaces) between the clusters.

    - Draw up the non-managerial efforts in the programme plan.

    - Carry out all those efforts that you have designated to the start-up stage.

Notes

- The GEM is the cornerstone of the programme.
- 'ER' goals can never be achieved, they are a direction to aim for.
- ER goals can be translated into MACIC (Measurable, Acceptable, Communicated, Inspiring, Committing,) or SMART (Specific, Measurable, Acceptable, Realisable, Traceable) goals; make sure this is done.

Checklist 10.2

Determine the Goals of Your Programme

The programme goals justify the programme's existence.

The ER goals specify what the programme is pursuing; greatER turnover, highER profits, lowER costs are examples of ER goals. These goals describe the desired characteristic of a specific object in its relevant environment.

A programme goal defines what the stakeholders are aiming to achieve.

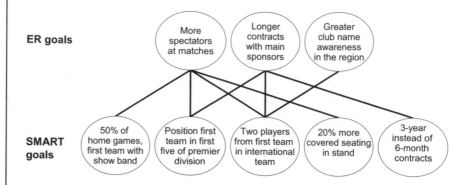

ER goals
- More spectators at matches
- Longer contracts with main sponsors
- Greater club name awareness in the region

SMART goals
- 50% of home games, first team with show band
- Position first team in first five of premier division
- Two players from first team in international team
- 20% more covered seating in stand
- 3-year instead of 6-month contracts

Figure 10.3   A single programme can pursue several (conflicting) goals

- *How to specify the goals of your programme:*
    - Determine the intentions, expectations and opinions of all those involved in the project.
    - Ensure that those involved all agree the significance of the programme.
    - Ensure that all those involved in the programme are fully aware of their own motives, expectations and opinions.
    - Specify the components of the programme's goals (the goal structure) and the relationships between them; find out all the relevant facts and figures and list the consequences if the goals are not pursued.
    - Clearly define the boundaries of the programme's goals and state what does not belong within these boundaries.
    - Ensure that the programme goals can be and are pursued.

Notes

- Programme goals indicate what must be pursued at any given moment.
- Goals can be described as the pursuit of an ideal: for example, a more profitable turnover from the sale of television sets, less crime in our village or greater efficiency in one of our departments.

- Ultimately, you need to demonstrate how the non-managerial efforts within the programme will bring the achievement of programme goals closer.

Checklist 10.3

Plan the Efforts for Each Stage of Your Programme

Only when a programme's goals have been adequately defined and its boundaries determined can any thought be given to the non-managerial efforts or stage activities, and the sequence necessary for pursuing them.

These efforts are drawn together in a plan. Your plan should not be overly restrictive: it is only designed to give an idea of how best the programme can be carried out, taking into account current thinking and your understanding of current and future circumstances. For this reason, such a plan is always more concrete for the immediate future. Insight and circumstances change over time, as does the plan, but it still has to be managed.

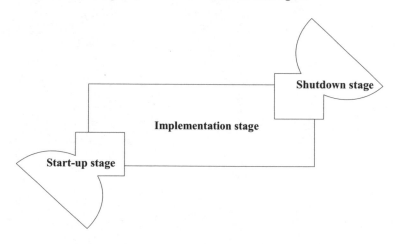

Figure 10.4 The three stages of a programme

- *How to plan the stage efforts of your programme:*

Programme efforts are described using verbs.

- Brainstorm all the non-managerial efforts that will be worthwhile, necessary or useful to help pursue the goals.

- You need to brainstorm from the perspective of your start point and then also work back from where you are trying to get to.

- Always do this together with those who will be doing the work.

- Determine a natural/logical sequence for these non-managerial efforts and identify any efforts which can be carried out at the same time (possibly by breaking them down into their constituent parts).

- Make sure that each description of an effort contains a verb.

- State any interim results and the end result of each effort.

- Specify the tools and materials, approach or method to be used for each effort.

Notes

- The stage (or content) plan for your programme only describes the non-managerial efforts; it does not describe management efforts or activities.
- Clustering efforts can be useful to help get an overview of programmes that contain a large number of efforts.
- The stage plan describes all the non-managerial efforts within the programme and not just the interesting ones or just those to be carried out by the programme organisation itself.

Checklist 10.4

Construct a Goals/Efforts/Means Network

The goals/efforts/means network (GEM) of a programme is as the name suggests made up of the goals, the efforts, the means and the interfaces between them.

A GEM can consist of a large number of bundled and linked projects and other efforts.

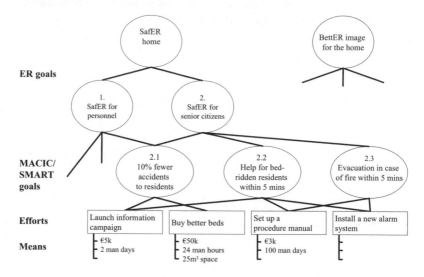

Figure 10.5 A goals/efforts/means network example

Constructing a GEM is a highly collaborative effort.

- **How to construct a GEM:**

  - Break down the top level goals into subsidiary goals.

  - Map out the interfaces between all the goals and their subsidiaries (a goals network).

  - Link the non-managerial efforts to the goals and state which efforts are expected to contribute to which goals.

  - List the priorities for the various goals and efforts.

  - Make an inventory of available and requisite means/resources.

  - Allocate available resources to the efforts on the basis of when they are required.

  - Make the GEM manageable; discuss it with all those involved and publish a final version.

Notes

- The GEM (goals/efforts/means network) is the cornerstone of every programme.
- Constructing a complete and balanced GEM is not a simple process.
- The ultimate purpose of a GEM is to gain an overview of the main goals as well as an insight into the subsidiary goals that support them.

Checklist 10.5

Construct Programme Clusters

By constructing programme clusters (subprogrammes), it is often possible to maintain a better overview of the whole programme. Clustering also offers insight into how different programme elements relate.

However, recognising clusters in a programme demands an unambiguous specification of all the relevant relationships between the clusters. You need to be vigilant to ensure that these interfaces are not changed, either accidentally or by unauthorised persons.

Structuring principle	The most important advantages (+) and disadvantages (-) of different programme structures
Organisation-oriented	+ Easy to delegate - Not cross-departmental
Sequential	+ Justifies the 'natural' sequence - Lead-times are sometimes excessive
Object-oriented	+ Promotes goal-orientation - Usually difficult to organise
Functional	+ Makes efficient use of scarce resources possible - Seldom does justice to an inter- or multidisciplinary programme
Financial	+ Simplifies the (financial) obligation of responsibility - Is usually not a natural or logical one
Market-oriented	+ Strengthens a customer-friendly approach - Does not always prevent duplication
Geographical	+ Makes it possible to use local resources - Can make communication difficult
Process-oriented	+ Prevents superfluous stocks and delays - Does not always follow the hierarchy
Mixed	+ All the advantages (?/!) - All the disadvantages (?/!)

Figure 10.6   Various programme structuring principles with their advantages and disadvantages

• *How to structure your programme:*

   • Choose one of the following methods: organisation-oriented, sequential, object-oriented, functional, financial, market-oriented, geographical, process-oriented or mixed.

   • Split the programme up into clusters according to the chosen structural category.

   • A cluster is a logically grouped number of non-managerial efforts and subsidiary goals within a programme where:

      – there is a relatively simple relationship between the groups;

- the relationship within the group is primarily based on experience, know-how and so on.
- Specify each cluster.
- Link each cluster to the goals being pursued.
- Specify all the relationships between the clusters, for example a common outcome or a physical relationship. But you should also specify the relationships between the other elements of your programme (goals, efforts, means).

Notes

- The greater the number of clusters, the greater the number of relationships that need to be maintained.
- The greater the number of clusters, the more opportunities for delegation and parallel working.
- The logical division of clusters will not always fit seamlessly into the structure of the existing permanent organisations taking part in the programme.

The whole is always more than the sum of its parts.

Checklist 10.6

Manage Your Programme

The primary programme management tasks include more general managerial activities such as inspiring and motivating people and initiating, coordinating and ending the routine activities within the programme.

This checklist highlights the most important branches of programme management: planning and progress control. These two branches of management are carried out with the help of the management perspectives: tempo, feasibility, efficiency, flexibility and goal-orientation (TFEFG).

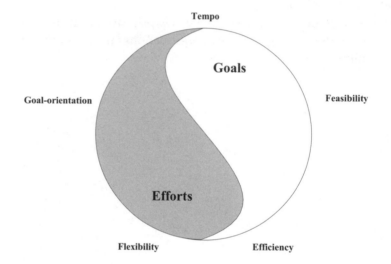

Figure 10.7   A programme needs five perspectives to be managed

- *Beware the following:*

  - The programme is put on hold for several months during each budget round, waiting for authorised financing.

  - Support for the programme has dwindled and yet it continues to run because people are afraid to lose face.

  - There are no remedial measures in place where they are really needed when things go awry.

  - Sometimes stakeholders don't want to have unambiguity in your programme because they then loose the freedom of going their own way.

  - The programme manager is basically no more than a programme coordinator.

- ### *The five management perspectives*

There are five important perspectives for managing a programme: tempo, feasibility, efficiency, flexibility and goal-orientation. Each of these perspectives must be managed independently and in conjunction with the other four.

- Tempo is the pace at which:
    - the agreed effects are realised;
    - the agreed efforts have been carried out;
    - the agreed capacity (manpower, means and facilities) are available.
- Feasibility is the probability of:
    - the agreed effects becoming evident in the future;
    - the efforts being carried out successfully;
    - the means becoming usable.
- Efficiency is the economic desirability of:
    - the agreed effects producing sufficient added value, financial or otherwise;
    - the efforts being carried out;
    - the cost of resources and the extent to which they have been made use of.
- Flexibility is the degree to which:
    - the agreed effects can be adapted (added to, eliminated, increased or decreased);
    - the relationships between efforts and between efforts and goals are adaptable;
    - efforts and the associated effects can be realised with increased or fewer means (manpower, resources and facilities).
- Goal-orientation is the degree to which:
    - the agreed effects make a direct or indirect contribution to the programme goals;
    - the efforts make a 'measurable' contribution to the agreed effects;
    - the use of resources, manpower and facilities contributes to the efforts and their outcome.

- ### *How to put the management perspectives into practice:*

- Get the most important players round the table.
- Evaluate the value of each programme goal and programme effort in terms of the management perspectives.
- Assign a desired quantitative value to each of the management perspectives.

STARTING AND
EXECUTING YOUR
PROGRAMME
– CHECKLISTS

- Based on this valuation, determine the relative value of each effort compared with the management perspectives.
- Balance the results until the desired programme of goals, efforts and means is achieved.
- To ensure a broad support base, involve all the relevant programme bodies in these decisions.
- Record the outcome and guard it against unauthorised changes.

Notes

- The management perspectives must be established for each individual programme.
- A management perspective gives direction to a programme.
- Integrated programme management requires a focus on the five management perspectives.

Checklist 10.7

Monitor Your Programme

A programme cannot be viewed in isolation. It is important to monitor the greatest, most significant changes to the environment carefully and regularly.

Monitoring usually requires specific measuring instruments to observe, recognise and assess the effects of a programme.

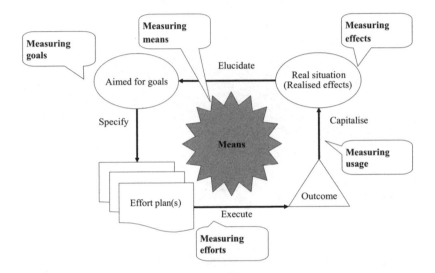

The outside world has a great influence on a programme.

Figure 10.8   There are several objects in a programme to be measured

- *How to monitor your programme:*

  - Determine what needs to be monitored; for example the relevant programme environment, the area to be influenced or the market you are trying to conquer.

  - Determine the effects to be monitored and the changes or developments that you are looking for (such as the growth or lessening of these effects).

  - Determine, develop and put in place the means for measuring, including the instruments and protocols, and details of the persons or bodies charged with carrying it out.

  - Transfer the results into a proposal for adjusting the GEM.

Notes

- Not all the effects are the result of the programme efforts.

- The person responsible for monitoring the programme observes, interprets and proposes adjustments.

- The more turbulent the environment, the greater the need for frequent and careful monitoring.

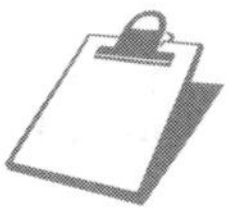

Checklist 10.8

Prioritise the Programme Efforts

It is not always possible or advisable to engage all the efforts in a programme simultaneously. Some efforts are dependent on the results of others, while others are so costly that they need to be postponed until required.

Because the programme environment is sometimes quite unstable, you need to regularly revise the priorities you gave to the different efforts.

What is important today is usually forgotten tomorrow.

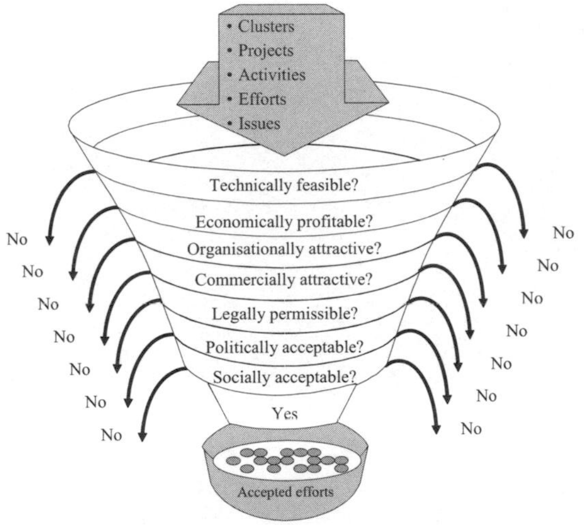

Figure 10.9 Many aspects have to be considered when prioritising efforts in a programme

- ***How to prioritise the efforts of your programme:***
  - Evaluate the comparative value of each of the management perspectives.
  - Estimate the contribution of each perspective to the non-managerial effort.
  - Multiply this contribution by the value of the perspectives to discover the effort's calculated priority.
  - Allow stakeholders to assess your priorities: do they agree with them on an emotional, intuitive and instinctive level?
  - If necessary, adjust the priorities on the basis of this subjective opinion.
  - Agree the circumstances under which these priorities should be revised.

Notes

- In a rapidly changing environment, the priorities must also be frequently revised.
- Having to change priorities too frequently is a sign of an unmanaged programme.
- It is ultimately the programme owner who can and must determine the priorities.

Checklist 10.9

Draw Up a Programme Plan

Planning or devising a plan is the first essential step in the decision-making process of programme management. This entails drawing up, approving and carrying out programme plans.

No plan – no progress control.

Planning in this sense is not restricted to time planning, but includes the planning of capacities (personnel), finances (profit and loss), performance and communication. As with any plan, a programme plan must address diverse areas and subjects.

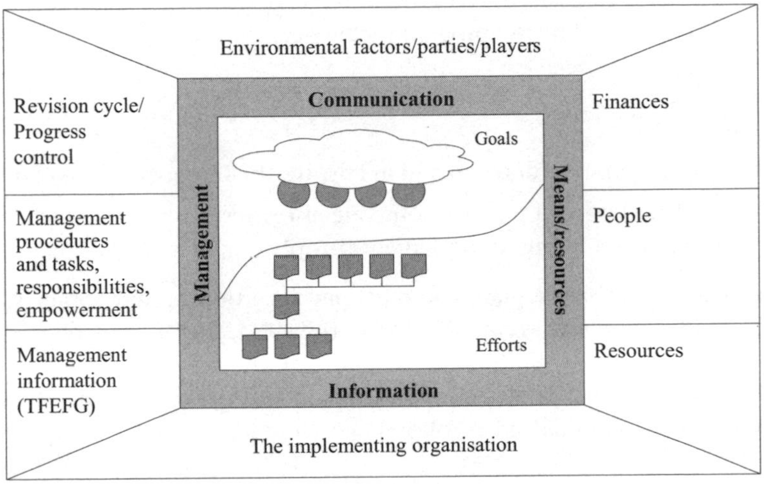

Figure 10.10   The structure of a complete programme plan

- ***How to draw up your programme plan:***

  - Determine the plan's target group; consider various versions of the plan for different groups.
  - Determine the plan's content; consider, for example:
    - the goals and the constituent sub-goals;
    - an overview of the non-managerial efforts;
    - the GEM;
    - the management criteria for each management perspective (including contingencies or margins) and the management plans;
    - the programme's organisation and communication;
    - the schedule, including capacities;
    - the financial plan;

- the plans for monitoring and progress control;
- the review plan.

- Evaluate the comparative value of each of the management perspectives.
- Multiply this value by the value of the criterion to discover the effort's contribution.
- Determine the aim of the plan: compiling reports for verification, internal communication or communication to third parties; it should be short and to the point or explanatory and informative. Then:
  - gather together the content;
  - draw up the plan;
  - discuss it with the stakeholders, explain it, adjust and so on;
  - following the agreed procedure, have the final version formally approved by the programme owner.

Notes

- Working together to draw up a plan ensures the integrity of the plan.
- Those who draw up a plan for someone else often encounter much resistance when trying to implement this plan.

In a complete programme plan, you must pay attention to nine subjects: the goals (including the management criteria), the GEM, the lifecycle plan, the financial plan, the contribution assessment plan, the organisation plan, the communication plan, the progress control plan and the review plan. These nine subjects are summarised as follows.

1   Goals

A programme plan contains the description of the specific and corresponding programme goals and objectives, and programme starting points (hypotheses). The interfaces between goals are also described here, bringing out for instance any elements that conflict and overlap.

2   GEM

The goals/efforts/means network (GEM) divides the set-up or structure of the programme into clusters, which make up projects, improvisation and routines that can be delegated. The GEM includes a clear and unambiguous description of all efforts, outcomes and interfaces. Also included are all the agreed means for every effort. The interfaces between the programme and its environment, between the different programme clusters, and also between the various projects and other work packages within each cluster should be covered in the GEM. The relationships that are agreed are essential for effectively managing the interfaces in your programme.

3 Lifecycle plan

The lifecycle plan of a programme tells you when all the projects and other activities of the programme are to be carried out. For each programme activity, the start date, conclusion date, allocated resources (such as personnel, materials and tools) and the sequence of events should be mentioned. A lifecycle plan should be as detailed as possible for the short term (the first six to twelve months), with limited contingencies. For the phases that follow (years), the planning is less detailed, with more generous contingencies, up to the planned end of the lifecycle of the programme.

4 Financial plan

The financial plan contains the required profitability (over time), available budgets, required financial resources and the returns and savings to be realised. This information is often summarised in a discounted cash-flow diagram for the whole lifecycle of the programme.

5 Contribution assessment plan

The contribution assessment plan is drawn up to assess all programme efforts and their outcomes in terms of the extent to which they contribute to the desired programme goals. For this purpose, unambiguous, programme-specific norms should be set (with contingencies or margins), stemming from the primary programme goals. One way to determine these norms or management criteria is by answering the question: what criteria will be used to evaluate the success of the programme? These success-determining norms should then be formulated to make them assessable and testable. In some cases, it may also be necessary to design an assessment tool for this purpose. Management criteria should:

- stem from the programme goals, often through the effects;
- be translated into efforts;
- be visible in terms of the resources (capacities, materials, tools, whether expressed in terms of money or not).

The most important data contained in this section are the specifications for the management criteria agreed in the programme, through which priorities within the programme are set and new activities selected.

6 Organisation plan

This section of the programme plan determines both the internal organisation of the programme and the relationships between the programme organisation and the relevant permanent organisations within its environment. The programme strategy has already been determined in the first two sections of the programme plan. In this section other organisational elements are added. These include:

- the management style to be adopted, such as the use of power, the type of management, the way conflicts are dealt with and the processes by which people will communicate and interact;

- the culture, which describes the way in which people get along, and the norms, symbols and rituals they use and share;

- personnel, which is not so much the numbers involved but rather their motivation and effort, and also the way in which teams are created and cooperate (including with external partners);

- organisation structure, which should address the questions: who is the programme's owner, who is the programme manager, who has overall responsibility, who is going to do what, who has authority, who may give approval, who should hold discussions with whom according to an established consultative structure?

7   Communication plan

The communication plan covers all sorts of regulations, tools and such like that are connected with the internal and external communication for the period of the programme, including: an overview of the communication goals, such as PR objectives, transfer of knowledge or influence for the various target groups, the communication media and channels, those responsible for the content as well as those who will actually be taking care of the communication.

8   Progress control plan

This section of the programme plan contains the description of the ways and the systems by which progress control and reporting will be carried out; who should report to whom, how often and in what way. The current situation regarding the management perspectives, criteria and plans can be found by looking at and evaluating the following aspects:

- effects realised;

- outcome of interim and final results;

- deployment of resources.

9   Review plan

The review cycle is presented in the last section of the programme plan. The review plan defines who, how (the procedure) and how often the programme plan will be reviewed, and how ad hoc requests for change will be dealt with.

Checklist 10.10

Carry Out the Implementation Stage

The implementation stage involves the actual pursuit of the programme goals through the planned non-managerial efforts.

Another important task is finishing the programme.

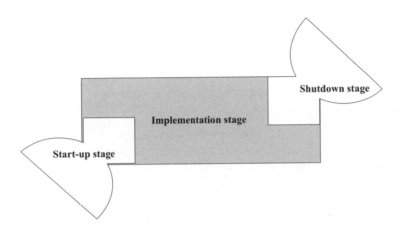

Figure 10.11   The implementation stage of a programme

- ***How to carry out the implementation stage of your programme:***
  - Make sure the non-managerial efforts are carried out.
  - Redefine the goals.
  - Identify any new or additional goals.
  - Adjust the part of the programme plan dealing with content.
  - Communicate the outcomes of the efforts, including the project results, to those who will use, keep and maintain them.
  - Draw up the final programme plan.

Notes

- The implementation stage can last for several years.
- Changes must be carefully controlled, during implementation.
- Anything not implemented can be completed during the shutdown stage.

Nothing is achieved without effective implementation.

Checklist 10.11

Carry Out the Shutdown Stage

This stage is part of the programme as such, and should be initiated with care.

Initiating shutdown is still part of the programme and involves integrating the programme into newly established or existing permanent organisations.

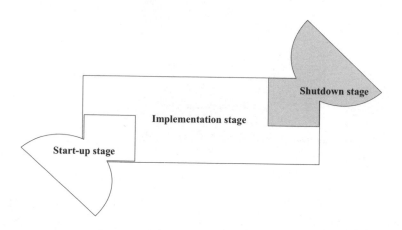

Figure 10.12 The shutdown stage of a programme

- ***How to carry out the shutdown stage of your programme:***

  - The shutdown stage should not last for ever.
  - Communicate the outcomes of these efforts, including the project results.
  - Enable the results to be used, supported and maintained.
  - Ensure that all programme results are formally handed over as agreed upon.
  - Ensure that all remaining resources are formally handed back.

Every programme must come to an end.

Notes

- The implementation stage can last for several years.
- By the shutdown stage, the outcomes of the results of the efforts should be apparent.
- When the programme has run its course it is closed down.

Glossary

Activity   An element of work performed during the course of a project.

Adjust   To adjust a project, programme or the latest version of a decision document or management plan to reflect the newest insights or situation.

Approve   Agreement to a decision or proposal by the person responsible in a controlled process. See also *Release*.

Assess the current situation   To determine the current state of a project or programme (what is now actually finished?).

Attune   To make clear and precise agreements about tasks, responsibilities and authority between the members of the project organisation and the existing organisation(s).

Authorise   To agree to a document as a basis for the continuation of project activities or programme efforts. See also *Release*.

Audit   The systematic, integral and independent evaluation of a project or programme.

Authority   The right to use and direct assigned resources within one's discretion to accomplish an assigned task.

Baseline document   A document that marks the border between two phases of a project containing:

*   a description of the (envisaged) project deliverable;
*   a summary of the activities to be carried out in subsequent phases;
*   and the relevant management plans.

Business case   Coherent/uniform image of the desired deliverable of a project, describing the justification for starting a project. This can be part of or output from the initiation phase.

Capacity   The amount of resources available or required to perform a project activity or a programme effort. In some methods also called effort.

Change   To change released decision documents or management plans according to a previously agreed procedure.

Change management   The process that leads to ensuring that all the consequences of a change being made to a decision document or management plan are known and accepted before they are actually implemented.

Checklist   An overview of steps or actions to be taken in (sub)processes of projects or programmes.

Commitment   Degree of agreement (the number of people who back a decision).

Communication   The contact that exists when two or more people send signals to, or receive signals from, each other.

Communication matrix   A matrix for a project or programme where the roles and tasks of those involved are recorded in certain (important) documents, such as minutes of meetings, reports, lists of appointments (excluding the decision documents or management plans).

Conflict   A situation where one person or party thinks that their concerns appear to be incompatible with those of another person or party.

Content activities/efforts   See *Phase activities* (non managerial activities or efforts).

Context   All the players and factors that can have a possible positive or negative influence on the project deliverable/result or programme outcome or course/path.

Context map   A map that describes the environment and the players within this environment, whether positive, neutral or negative, and their relationship to the project or programme. The map also lists the most important members/parties and their roles.

Control cycle   A periodic assessment where the management requirements (norms), with margins or contingencies, are compared to the actual state of affairs within the project or programme. When expected deviations are found amendments should be made to the (envisaged) deliverable or outcome. If this is no longer possible, the management plans should be amended in consultation with the project owner.

Corrective action   A managerial activity to ensure that the actual situation in which a project or programme finds itself is in agreement with the latest decision document or management plan.

Cost management   A model to keep track of the money planned/spent/budgeted/contracted/obligated and the remaining budget. Also a tool for the money management aspect. It should give insight to the money provided for, not yet spent; available; not yet spent, but (contractually) agreed; the remaining budget.

Culture   The behaviour of people within an organisation, based on common and current values and norms.

Decision document   See *Baseline document.*

Decision making   The integral choice/authorisation/acceptance/approval/release of each phase or stage of that which has actually been achieved (the description of the deliverable/goals and the content plan) from the management plans then available.

Define   To unequivocally determine what belongs to the project deliverable or result and what does not.

Definition phase   The phase where the requirements (external interfaces, functional and operational requirements and design constraints) of the project deliverable or result (and the goals behind it) and the activities of the project path are assessed, determined and recorded.

Delegate   To transfer authority but maintain responsibility.

Delegated project or programme owner   The person who operates in the name of the project or programme owner and has the same authority or is in a position to mobilise this authority.

Deliverable   A tangible or intangible, verifiable object that must be produced to complete a project. Also known as result, service, product, item, object, outcome or output.

Design constraint   The desired characteristic of the project result as envisaged by the 'maker'.

Documentation   Recorded project or programme data.

Duration   The number of work periods required to complete an activity.

Efficiency management   Ensuring that goals are pursued at the least possible cost, for the highest possible return.

Effort   A programme activity.

Elapsed time   Period already used.

ER goals/objectives   The desired state, quality or characteristic of an object in a specific environment; an unattainable ideal worth striving for. BettER consultation within our committee, a nicER building for our accommodation and friendliER behaviour from our receptionists to our clients are examples of this.

Estimate   Based on insight and experience, stating before an activity takes place what effort and what capacity and means will be necessary to bring it to completion.

Evaluate   To judge a project or programme critically and systematically. A critical, well-ordered retrospective of a project or programme (what went well, what could have been better, what has to be done differently, and so on).

External interfaces   The requirements of the project that must be met unconditionally. These requirements are laid down by law and by the environment of the (intended) project deliverable/result.

Failure factor   The possible reason for the failure of a project or programme.

Failure factor analysis   An investigation into the factors that have such a negative influence on a project's or programme's success (deliverable/outcome and/or path) that they could cause the project or programme to fail. This investigation should lead to measures that can reduce, prevent or avoid these risks.

Feasibility management   The responsibility for taking the measures necessary to ensure that the (programme) goals can, in all probability, be striven for.

Feasibility study   An analysis to determine if a project is viable, if the success of the project is probable and if the deliverable of the project is realisable.

Feedback   Offering an opinion on how certain behaviour is experienced by others to the person displaying this behaviour.

Flexibility management   Ensuring that the programme (the programme's goals), the efforts and means, contain sufficient margins.

Functional boss or supervisor   The one who determines the way in which the project or programme team member carries out his task and bears the responsibility for his or her professional development.

Goal   The desired state, quality or characteristic of an object in a specific environment; an unattainable ideal worthwhile pursuing. Also called objective, target, benefit, effect and outcome.

Goal-oriented management   Ensuring that the (programme) goals are pursued.

Hierarchical boss or supervisor   The person delegated by the permanent organisation who is responsible for the welfare of the individual project or programme team member and bears the responsibility for their personal development.

Improvise   A way of working where the outcome of activities or efforts is unpredictable because no one has sufficient authority to influence the process in a decisive manner.

Information matrix   A matrix within which the tasks, responsibilities and authority of each role in a project or programme are listed, with regard to the release of and changes to the decision document or management plan for that project or programme.

Lead time   See *Duration*.

MACIC   An acronym used for goals that are Measurable, Acceptable, Committing, Inspiring and Communicated.

Manage   To plan and control progress of the management aspects of a project (time, money, quality, information and organisation) or programme (tempo, flexibility, efficiency, feasibility and goal-orientation).

Margin   An indication of the accuracy of estimates regarding management plans available to the management of a project or programme to enable management to control the risks inherent to it and adequately anticipate uncertainties.

Means   Everything that will be used in a project or programme. There are various types of means like: tools, equipment, manpower, materials, power, energy or parts.

Milestone   The point in time when a clearly recognisable product or in-between deliverable is realised or produced (an interim deliverable, for instance) and real progress is seen.

Money management Financial management of costs, benefits/savings is necessary to carry out all the project activities responsibly and efficiently to ensure the profitability of the project result.

Monitor The management task, within the relevant environment of a programme, to observe which effects have already been achieved, whether these are a deliverable/result of the programme or not.

Multi-project management Managing a (large) number of projects simultaneously. These projects don't have a relevant coherence to be managed as such, but they do have to be executed by one resource.

Non-managerial activities or efforts Work that by its nature and in fact is essential to achieving the project deliverable or result or pursuing the programme goals; if this type of work is not carried out, the project deliverable cannot be (completely) achieved or the programme goals cannot be (sufficiently) pursued. Sometimes called phase or stage activities.

Operational boss or supervisor The person who determines what a project or programme team member must do.

Operational requirement A requirement made as to the use, care and maintenance of the project deliverable or result. How intensively the result must be used, kept and maintained.

Organisation form The agreed sharing of power between the temporary organisation, set up for a project or programme, and the permanent organisation(s) involved.

Organisation management The allocation of tasks, responsibilities and authority necessary to ensure that the people responsible for and authorised to carry out all the project activities or programme efforts do this in such a way that it leads to a formal accepted project result or programme outcome.

Owner The single individual with overall responsibility for ensuring that a project or programme meets its objectives and delivers the projected benefits. The project owner can enforce, protect and facilitate it. Executive, customer, client are often used alternative terms.

Parent (or existing) organisation(s) Existing organisation(s) within which, or between which, projects or programmes are carried out.

Performance requirement The characteristics of the project deliverable (or result) demanded by the project owner. In order that the deliverable will and can be used to pursue the goals and to diminish the problems.

Permanent organisation   The group of people who have agreed to pursue the organisation's goals for an indefinite period. See also *Parent organisation*.

Perspective   A distinctive way of looking at a project by management. It contains planning and progress control. There are five management perspectives in a project. These perspectives are project time management, project money management, project quality management, project release management and project organization management.

Phase   A collection of logically related project activities, usually culminating in the completion of a (in-between) deliverable.

Phase activity   Any piece of non-managerial work, necessary for achieving the project result, performed during the course of a project.

Phasing   Determining and carrying out the activities (in the correct order) necessary for achieving the project result.

Plan   To ensure that all those concerned with a project or programme, and especially the team members, are informed what has to be done, within which margins, in which order and why, by means of management plans. This is a management task.

Planning   The management planning of a project or programme. Occasionally, the term planning is only understood to mean time planning. An overview of the estimated quantities necessary for the project or programme (time, money, capacity, material and so on).

Power   The potential ability to influence behaviour, to change the course of events, to overcome resistance, and to get people to do things that they would not do otherwise.

Prioritise   The importance of certain activities (in a project) or efforts (in a programme) in relation to other activities or efforts mentioned. This can find expression in an (earlier) required completion date and the allocation of (extra) means.

Programme   A programme is a unique complex of goals, goal-oriented efforts, including projects, which must be carried out with limited means.

Programme cluster   A group of efforts that for some reason 'logically' belong together within a programme.

Programme content   The actual goals and all the constituent (logical) efforts necessary to pursue them.

Programme context map   A map that describes the environment and the players within this environment, whether positive, neutral or negative, and their relationship to the programme. The map also lists the most important members/parties regarding the programme and their role.

Programme goals   Everything that is pursued with the help of the programme. Sometimes called objectives.

Programme management   The management (planning, progress control and monitoring) of a programme.

Programme management perspectives (or criteria)   Tempo, feasibility, efficiency, flexibility and goal-orientation.

Programme office   Support function/department for the programme manager charged with administrative activities (compiling and sending reports, archiving and so on). Also, an organisation offering support in the carrying out of a programme, especially aimed at supporting management tasks.

Progress control   To ensure that what is stated in the management plans is actually carried out within the given margins.

Progress report   An interim written report stating the progress that has been made and what this has required. It will also give an insight into the feasibility of the activities/efforts still to be completed compared with the management plans in question.

Project   A project is a jointly predetermined unique result or deliverable that must be realised with limited means and a unique complex of activities.

Project brief   A description of the project at the end of the initiation phase containing the description of the deliverable, the activities (work) and the management plans. It is the starting point of the definition phase. Sometimes a business case is part of the project brief.

Project content   The project deliverable and all the necessary, logical, natural activities for achieving it. It is the non-managerial side of the project.

Project management   A balanced application of knowledge, skills, tools and attitudes with respect to environment, key players, interaction and method to realise the project deliverable.

Project managing   Managing (planning and progress control) of the five project management aspects of a project. Also called project management.

Project management perspectives   Time, money, quality, release, organisation.

Project manager   The individual responsible for managing a project.

Project office   Support function/department for the project manager charged with administrative activities (compiling and sending reports, archiving and so on). Also, an organisation offering support in the carrying out of a project, especially aimed at supporting management tasks.

Project path   The sum of all content activities that are carried out to achieve the project deliverable/result. See also *Project plan.*

Project phase   A collection of logically related non-managerial project activities, usually starting on and culminating in a decision document.

Project phases   Initiation, definition, design, preparation, realisation and follow-up phase. All these phases have their own objective and a set of non-managerial activities.

Project plan   A document where all the content, or non-managerial activities that will be carried out are recorded in a logical and natural order.

Project start-up   A structured meeting by the (intended) project team aimed at drafting the project's initial starting document (the project brief or business case) – in concept form.

Quality management   Ensuring that the project deliverable meets the quality requirements and that all the project activities are carried out in such a way as to meet the requirements of the project deliverable/result. Quality requirements are measurable (non-managerial) requirements. Quality management consists of the formulation of quality requirements, the drafting of a quality plan, the monitoring of quality progress (by way of testing, assessment and evaluation) and adjustment.

Quality requirement   A measurable non-managerial requirement of the project deliverable that is in some way evident or can be proven, that is present in the project (or the future) project deliverable/result.

Reference group   A group of people who can be asked to critically evaluate or react to a proposal (concept plan).

Release   Release management is the identification, registration and control of data necessary to ensure that all project activities are carried out in the required and agreed way and that the project deliverable (or result) is recorded unambiguously. Some call this configuration and change management. See also *Decision making.*

Requirements A set of the content-related needs, desires or wishes that the project deliverable or result must meet. Management requirements are not included.

Resource See *Means*.

Resource management Planning and control of resources.

Responsibilities Matters that someone can be held to account for.

Risk See *Failure factor analysis*.

Risk analysis An investigation into the potential failure factors in a project or programme and the measures proposed for their identification and, if possible, neutralisation. See also *Failure factor analysis*.

Risk management The entire set of activities and measures that are aimed at dealing with risks in order to maintain control over a project or programme.

Routine A repeated series of activities that, when using the same means each time, always produces an identical result/product/service or deliverable.

Schedule A plan of activities/efforts placed within a time frame.

Scope The sum of products and services to be provided as one project deliverable.

SMART An acronym used for goals that are Specific, Measurable, Acceptable, Realisable and Traceable.

Sponsor The person who provides support and encouragement and protects the project or programme and, where possible, provides useful advice. Usually a figure of authority within the participating organisation(s).

Stage A collection of logically related programme efforts, usually culminating in the required outcome.

Status report See *Progress report*.

Steering group An advisory group to the project or programme owner that meets to discuss (the progress reports of) decision documents or programme plans. The owner, who is often the chairman of the steering group or committee, always has the final word.

Structure   To give a project or programme a logical form by splitting it into parts in such a way that an insight into the project or programme content and the general picture of it is given.

Subproject   A smaller portion of the overall project. It is a logical group of activities within a project, where the coherence with other subprojects is relatively simple.

Support (staff)   People maintaining and administering a project deliverable (on behalf of the owner and end users of the deliverable) during the follow-up phase.

Team   A group of people with complementary skills, dedicated to achieving mutual goals and who use an agreed working method for which they take joint responsibility.

Team building   The process or activity that forges the team into one cooperative unit.

Team member   A person charged with carrying out activities within a project or efforts within a programme.

Team role   A tendency to behave, contribute and interrelate with others in a particular way. Having the freedom to use one's talents.

Tempo management   Ensuring sufficient speed within the programme whereby goals are pursued within the margins of a stipulated timeframe with the means available.

Temporary organisation   The form of cooperation for a project or programme.

Testing   Checking the extent to which the (interim) deliverable/result meets the stated requirements. Sometimes called assessing, controlling, evaluating, inspecting or verifying.

Time management   Ensuring that all non-managerial project activities are carried out on time with the resources available thus ensuring that the project deliverable does not fall outside the margins of the schedule.

User(s)   The person or group who will use the deliverable of the project or the outcome of a programme.

Bibliography

Belbin, M.R. (1996), *Team roles at work* (Oxford: Butterworth-Heinemann).

Bennis, W. (1999), *Managing people is like herding cats* (Provo: Executive Excellence Publishing).

Blanchard, K. et al. (1990), *The one minute manager builds high performing teams* (New York: William Morrow & Company).

Bossidy, L. and Charan, R. (2002), *Execution; the discipline of getting things done* (New York: Crown Business).

Carroll, T. (2006), *Project delivery in business-as-usual organisations* (Aldershot: Gower Publishing).

CCTA (2002), *Managing successful projects with Prince2* (London: The Stationery Office).

Covey, S.R. (1991), *Principle-centered leadership* (New York: Fireside).

Covey, S.R. (2004), *The 8th habit* (New York: Free Press).

Davis, T. and Pharro, R. (2003), *The relationship manager* (Aldershot: Gower Publishing).

Fullan, M. (2001), *Leading in a culture of change* (San Francisco: Jossey-Bass).

Goleman, D., Boyatzis, R. and McKee, A. (2002), *Primal leadership: Realizing the power of emotional intelligence* (Boston: Harvard Business School Press).

Harvard Business Review (ed.) (1989), *Managing projects and programmes* (Boston: Harvard Business School Press).

Hersey, P., Blanchard, K. and Johnson, D. (2000), *Management of organizational behaviour* 8th Edition. (Prentice Hall).

Hofstede, G. and Hofstede, G.J. (2004), *Cultures and organizations – software of the mind* (New York: McGraw-Hill).

Katzenbach, J.R. and Smith, D.K. (1993), *The wisdom of teams* (Boston: Harvard Business School Press).

Kerzner, H. (1998), *In search of excellence in project management* (New York: John Wiley & Sons).

Landsberg, M. (1998), *The Tao of coaching* (London: Harper Collins Publishers).

Lencioni, P. (2005), *Overcoming the five dysfunctions of a team* (San Francisco: Jossey-Bass).

Peters, T. (2005), *Tom Peters essentials: Leadership* (London: Dorling Kindersley Limited).

Pfeffer, J. (1992), *Managing with power; politics and influence in organizations* (Boston: Harvard Business School Press).

Project Management Institute, Inc. (2004), *A Guide to the project management body of knowledge* (Pennsylvania: Project Management Institute, Inc.).

Thomas, K.W. and Kilmann, R.H. (1974), *Thomas Kilmann conflict mode instrument* (Tuxedo NY: Xicom).

Tuckman, B.W. (1965), 'Developmental Sequence in Small Groups', *Psychological Bulletin* 63, 384–399.

Well-Stam, D., Van Lindenaar, F., Van Kinderen, S. and Van den Bunt, B. (2004), *Project risk management; An essential tool for managing and controlling projects* (London: Kogan Page Limited).

Wijnen, G. and Kor, R. (1999), *Managing unique assignments* (London, Gower).

Wijnen, G. and Kor, R. (2005), *Managing projects and programs* (Nankai Xiandai Xiangmu).

Zenger, J.H., Musselwhite, E., Hurson, K. and Perrin, C. (1993), *Leading teams: Mastering the new role* (New York: McGraw-Hill).

Index

About the Authors

Rudy Kor and Gert Wijnen are management consultants with Twynstra Gudde Consultants and Managers, an international, independent, result-oriented and pragmatic consultancy firm with over 500 employees. They both are specialised in project and programme management. For some decades they have assisted in starting up, auditing and assessing projects and programmes. They have trained thousands of people in project and programme management and helped them to professionalise their approach to managing projects and programmes.

Both authors have acquired experience in industrial and service organisations in the private and public sector. They have published some hundred articles on the subjects of organising, general management, project and programme management and leadership. They are authors or co-authors of thirteen books. One of their books has been translated into Chinese.

Rudy and Gert are convinced that their project as well as their programme approach are very useful in small, teamwork-oriented assignments of some months (usually managed by a part-time project or programme manager). But the basic ideas of both approaches have also proven to be applicable to big, multi-billion-euro assignments of several years managed by full-time managers.